Stop E.
Start Living

Stop Existing, Start Living

Help Yourself Take Control of Your Life Through Hypnotherapy

CHRISTINE WOOLFENDEN

DARTON·LONGMAN + TODD

First published in Great Britain in 2017 by
Darton, Longman and Todd Ltd
1 Spencer Court
140 – 142 Wandsworth High Street
London SW18 4JJ

ISBN 978–0–232–53284–5

A catalogue record for this book is available from the British Library

Produced by Judy Linard
Printed and bound in Great Britain by Bell & Bain, Glasgow

To Charlie

Contents

List of audio cues

Acknowledgements

Where this book is concerned, there are many people to whom I'm incredibly grateful. Most of all I'd like to thank my trusted friends and family who believed in me sufficiently to take the time out of their busy lives to read and comment on the multiple drafts. Their constructive feedback and unending support gave me the confidence to take this project forward. Amongst these people I especially thank my husband, Charlie, my two daughters, Tess and Billie, my mother, Eleanor, my friends Sarah, Diane, Sue, Rod and Helen, my sister Liz, my nephew Joe and my cousin Loopy. And then there's John, without whose publishing expertise I would have been lost.

I'd also like to thank Darton, Longman and Todd for having the vision to publish this book, and to Nicola of The Institute of Clinical Hypnosis for her thorough and stimulating hypnotherapy training.

Please consider yourselves well and truly appreciated.

To whom it may concern

Duncan sat alone at the edge of the worn single bed at his parents' house, head in hand. At 41, this was the last place on earth he wanted to be. On the floor, in between the cardboard boxes that contained his possessions, was a local advertiser, the pages randomly opened. A word caught his eye. It read 'change'. For him, it was a light-bulb event, a moment of clarity that over-powered his tolerance of the status quo, prompted action and led him to my door.

What is it, I wonder, that's led *you* here to these words on this page?

It could be curiosity, a desire to know more about hypnotherapy, perhaps a sense of obligation to a long-suffering friend who bought you a copy.

Or maybe, just maybe, you're fed up with robotically trudging your way through life and have had enough of merely getting by. Perhaps you're tired of those uneasy, niggling feelings of discomfort and dissatisfaction, and are wondering what the heck you can do about it.

I wholeheartedly welcome every one of you; especially those who fall within the latter category, for you stand to gain most of all.

Proviso
This book is not intended for individuals who have suffered abusive, violent or traumatic experiences, nor

would I recommend people follow this process if they've been diagnosed with a mental disorder. Instead, when you feel the time is right, I advise you to seek bespoke, face-to-face advice and support with a professional clinical hypnotherapist or a therapist from a preferred client-centred discipline.

Also, if the questions posed in each chapter of the book or the audio recordings that accompany this publication raise unbearably strong emotions, I advise you to stop and seek one-on-one professional guidance.

Preface

In 1955, the British Medical Association (BMA) issued a report stating that hypnosis was a valuable medical tool, and recommended that all new doctors be trained in applying it. Despite this endorsement, hypnosis has since become a much maligned, misrepresented and misunderstood form of psychological treatment. Because of this, hypnotherapy is often seen as the last option; 'I've tried everything else and nothing's worked so let's throw caution to the wind and give it a shot' – self-defeating. Or, it's seen as something with magical properties, a method that can change our behaviour whether we want it to or not by forces that lie beyond our control and human understanding – frightening and disempowering. Or it's simply seen as light entertainment.

Based on my experience to date and a mountain of evidence that hypnotherapy is an enduringly effective form of psychological treatment, one of the three aims of this book is to disentangle the nonsense from the reality where hypnotherapy is concerned, and to put hypnosis back on the map as a bona fide, enduringly effective client-centred therapy.

Furthermore, recent neuro-scientific advancement has led to a far greater understanding of how human brains function. The findings have provided invaluable evidence to support the theoretical foundations of hypnotherapy. With this in mind, the second aim of this book is to unite this current scientific knowledge with the theory and practice of hypnotherapy.

However, not surprisingly, the chief aim of this publication is to help you identify, understand and address the causes of your own dissatisfaction with life, and to enable you to stop existing and start living the life you choose to live.

There are five underlying premises to this book:
- First, with sufficient motivation to do so, human beings are capable of changing.
- Second, hypnotherapy is a safe and effective way of helping people change.
- Third, identifying the root cause of the problem and resolving those issues leads to the most enduring and beneficial form of change.
- Fourth, the key to successful change is self-responsibility. (Getting this straight from the outset, I can't make you do anything – only you can do that.)
- Fifth, the happiest, most fulfilled people are those who both know who they are and accept themselves for who they are.

The therapy contract

Every clinical hypnotherapist has their own style and methodology when it comes to helping people overcome their problems. What is detailed in this book represents my approach to problem resolution, a method of practice that I have refined over time.

I will not, alas, be available to you in person. One-to-one sessions with a qualified clinical hypnotherapist that you like and trust are, in my opinion, the most beneficial form of hypnotherapeutic treatment you can get. You just can't beat the luxury of one-to-one, focused help. But, such sessions generally appear expensive (it can feel hard to justify spending a considerable amount of money on yourself, particularly at a time of global economic instability) and often require time off work to attend – a double-whammy.

But, what I do offer within the pages of this book and the accompanying audios is my knowledge, knowledge gained from working with many clients for over ten years. You will be guided step by step through a development programme that will enable you to make changes at your own pace, changes that will assist you in understanding and relieving those feelings of discomfort and dissatisfaction, and help you achieve a greater sense of control and effectiveness in your life.

And, what are my expectations of you? Well, to be completely frank, I'm expecting a lot. To follow this process will require time, hard work, persistence and commitment (not to mention access to the internet to download the audios, many sheets of paper and multiple ink-filled pens). Plus, it's vital to understand from the very beginning of this process that the key to successful change is self-responsibility. With this in mind, in following this procedure, I am asking you to agree to take personal responsibility for the outcome.

The questions marked in **grey** are for you to work through yourself. When you first encounter these questions, they might seem rather demanding. In some ways, they are; they have been intentionally designed to encourage you to stop and think. But do not be put off by them; the more accurate self-knowledge you have, the better able you will be to make advantageous decisions about yourself and your life. So, I recommend you take your time to address each question – see it as an investment of your time, an investment in yourself – reflect, make notes and re-assess your responses. Then recognise the relevance of each response in relation to the discomfort and dissatisfaction you're currently feeling. If you come across a question that seems just too difficult to tackle, leave it for a while and come back to it later.

Positive change improves lives, but the path to change can, at times, feel uncomfortable and arduous, and setbacks can feel alarming. But, these difficulties are a very normal part of the change process. I ask you to stick with it. In fact, it's often the issues that we struggle over most that can result in the most profound change.

Make a decision; is now the right time to embark

on this project? Are you willing to fully commit to this process? Yes? Great. Then let's get going. (If the answer is a firm 'no' to both questions, place this book on your 'to be reviewed' shelf and re-visit it regularly. And, if you're hesitant in answering 'yes' to either question, gently ask yourself why this is the case and see if you can steer yourself toward a more definitive answer.)

Some introductions

1. *The thought of change can feel intimidating, but an understanding of what's involved in the process of change tends to ease trepidation.* So, first off, I'd like to introduce you to the development plan I'm offering, detailing how the procedure you are about to embark upon will unfold.

   Included with this book are 10 downloadable mp3 hypnosis recordings, recordings of my voice backed by gentle, soothing music. To access these audios please go to:

   > www.helpyourselfhypnotherapy.com;
   > name: helpyourself; password: takecontrol.

   Each audio is specifically engineered to help you comfortably relax, observe, learn and adjust. *Audio 1 – Good night, sleep well – is designed to be a part of your daily routine from the outset, its chief aim being to accustom you to the relaxing hypnotic state. From now until completion of this process (and beyond if you choose to), listen to the audio every night whilst lying in bed, ready for sleep. Should you fall asleep whilst listening to it, that's all right.*

Each subsequent hypnosis audio lasts about an hour, so, when an audio (look for this symbol 🎧) is cued within a chapter, please set aside about 60 minutes to listen to it, at a time when you're neither too tired nor likely to be disturbed. Then, find a warm, comfortable and safe place to lie back and begin relaxing.

I'm sure I don't need to say this, but, please do not multi-task whilst listening to the audios (no driving, no ironing, no 'I'll just pop it on in the background while I assemble my latest flat-pack') – they require your undivided attention. Also, for the same reason, please don't listen to the audios at times when you're under the influence of alcohol or drugs.

Experience tells me that people benefit greatly from understanding the concepts that underlie the therapeutic process, so, the first two chapters of this book are somewhat theoretical in nature. Chapters 1 and 2 centre on descriptions of how the incredible human mind generates our behaviour, what hypnotherapy is and how it works.

Where change is concerned, we can often, inadvertently, get in the way of our own progress. Therefore, Chapter 3 investigates possible mental attitudes to change that could impede *your* progress, attitudes such as 'change is frightening' and 'I can't change; I was born this way'.

Beginning the process of change, Chapter 4 focuses directly on you and your sense of ineffectiveness and discomfort in the present. Initially your definition of the presenting issue is explored with a view to gaining a clear understanding of what your discomfort is and how it's affecting your current life. Your goal state (how you'd prefer to feel) is then thought through and cemented via a hypnosis audio. Chapter 5 continues the process of change by exploring and re-educating that old sense of discomfort.

The reflection required to thoroughly investigate your current dissatisfaction with life might well seem a tad demanding, so Chapter 6 is designed to give you a breather from self-contemplation and provide you with a technique to generate a feeling of calm comfort at will.

More often than not, the problem with which people present is a symptom of something broader. To explore further layers of the issue, Chapters 7 to 9 address potential historical influences on your sense of discomfort, identifying and transforming unhelpful core beliefs, and exploring the possibility of moving beyond the influence of past experiences through a process of forgiveness.

Given that the value of self-knowledge cannot be overstated, Chapter 10 centres on investigating how well you really know yourself, helping you to not only understand who you are and what resources you have at your disposal, but also to then apply that knowledge to useful effect.

Chapter 11 acts as a summary of progress to date. And, finally, Chapter 12 provides you with the gift of self-hypnosis – a tool that you can use for the rest of your life, enabling you to become far more self-reliant in future problem-solving situations.

Please be aware that this is a process throughout

which your definition of the discomfort and dissatisfaction you feel will probably change. Once some aspects of a problem have been dealt with, it's very normal to begin unconsciously redefining the issue. To keep you on track, at the end of each chapter is a 'Progress report' – a brief outline of my expectations of your progress to date, followed by an opportunity for you to assess what you've *actually* learned, to then apply that knowledge directly to your original problem.

I also want to draw your attention to the possibility that, in the early stages, the more you unravel something, the worse it can feel. Rest assured, this is temporary; you *will* come out the other side. Just keep going.

2. *Hearing about other people's life experiences can be very beneficial, particularly when those experiences resonate with your own.* So, let me now introduce you to two very important people: Mia and Duncan (not their real names, of course).

Mia and Duncan represent clients of mine who, at different times, came to see me, presenting with a feeling that they were being ineffective in their lives, that they were existing, not living. They felt ill at ease within themselves and uncomfortable with the way that their lives were turning out.

Born in 1967, Duncan was a single 41-year-old IT specialist, working for a large organisation.

Mia, born in 1980, was a 30-year-old full-time mother of two children, married for 10 years to Geoff.

You will hear much more about Mia and Duncan throughout the book.

3.   And, last but not least, introducing me; for the next while, we're going to be in each other's company, so, just as if we were meeting in person for the first time, I'd like you to begin to feel comfortable with me. Let me describe myself a little.

You'll probably have seen my photo on the cover of this book; make of my appearance what you will. I do my best! I smile – a lot; it's a comfortable facial expression for me. My eyes are kind. I have a firm but not crippling handshake. I'm 53-years-old, am quite tall for my sex and am relatively slim – my weight goes up and down depending on the time of year and the amount of socialising I've done. I'm normal – imperfect – human! In my work role I dress smartly, but comfortably, choosing muted colours that, hopefully, add no distraction to the meeting. Much as I might choose to wear tracksuit bottoms or bedeck myself in jewels in my time off, during work, as far as I'm concerned, the office is a professional, bling-free zone.

I work from home. On arriving, you'd enter through the front door into the hallway, a large space decorated with artefacts collected from my time travelling in Namibia and Zimbabwe, and then, through to the office, a door just off the hallway.

My office is a compact and comfortable space, the walls festooned with my various professional certificates, the shelves stacked with books that relate to my profession – I read around my subject a lot. The purpose of the certificates is to reassure clients that I'm suitably trained in my field. Being the thorough sort of person that I am, once I had made the decision to re-train to become a clinical hypnotherapist, I went back to University and studied for a Graduate Diploma in Psychology. I then went to London to train with the Institute of Clinical Hypnosis (ICH). In 2006 I passed my Advanced Diploma in Hypnotherapy and Psychotherapy. I set up practice as a clinical hypnotherapist later that year and continue in this role to this day, regularly taking further instruction in my field of work to broaden and refresh my knowledge-base and skills. I take such pleasure in what I do.

There are also a couple of family photos in my office, so, if I were asked about them by a client, I would happily explain that I have two very loving and supportive parents, that I am married and have a step son, a daughter-in-law and a grandchild, and that I have two daughters, both now independent, magnificent young women.

Being a last-born child, my empathy for and respect of others developed from a young age. As I grew, I also acquired a very British sense of humour, seeing a tinge of lightness even in the darkest of situations. I regularly apply humour to my work, finding that laughter provides immense physical and psychological benefits to both me and my clients. I hope that these aspects of my character become evident as the book progresses.

That's enough about me. Now let's focus on you.

Stop Existing,
Start Living

Chapter 1

The utterly amazing human mind and how it generates our behaviour

Before we think further about the discomfort and dissatisfaction that's brought you here, it's interesting to begin to understand why we, as human beings, do what we do and sometimes continue to do what we're doing, even when we can see it's not constructive.

When we're feeling discomfort within our own lives, we often find ourselves doing things (taking drugs, smoking, procrastinating, over-eating, avoiding, drinking too much) that we know, at a rational level, are not going to really improve matters.

As soon as Mia got the children to bed she would dive straight to the fridge and pour herself a large glass of wine. Duncan ate chocolate, bars of it.

Why do we do this to ourselves when we know it's not good for us in the long run, and certainly won't genuinely resolve our problems? It seems ridiculous doesn't it? Illogical. Almost as though we were being impelled to behave in this way by some alien force.

So what's going on here? What is controlling our

behaviour? The answer is our minds, and the neural activity ocurring within them. But, how?

As discussed in *The Brain* by David Eagleman (2015), there are two parts to the human mind: the conscious and the unconscious, each playing a very different role in fashioning our behaviour.

In relation to our everyday behaviour, as intelligent people, there is a tendency, perhaps even a desire, to believe that we are rational, analytical, flexible individuals who spend our waking lives wielding our willpower in the conscious mode, fully aware of what we're doing and why we're doing it, making decisions and solving problems in the here and now based on available facts. *I'm afraid not.* The conscious mind is far too weak to achieve all these things. It simply doesn't have the capacity.

The conscious mind begins developing from about the age of two. It is akin to the mayor of a massive city of residents. It's the part that deals with life in the moment, and, based on information attended to and received via the five senses, gets involved when unexpected things happen and when we need to work out what short-term tactical move to make next.

The conscious mind, the mayor, also has a strategic overview of what's best for us in the long-term and has the capacity, via willpower, to steer behaviour away from possible detrimental activities towards behaviour that is in line with its long-term goals.

Wonderful. Let's just say 'no' to that glass of wine or bar of chocolate then and be done with it. This can be effective on occasions, but such conscious control of behaviour cannot be relied upon. The truth is, the resources of the conscious mind are easily depleted, and when our energy levels are low, our willpower doesn't stand a chance.

In terms of why we do what we do, and continue to do what we're doing, the vast majority of our behaviour stems from programmes running in the *unconscious* mind. Our behaviour typically becomes so automatic that we can't easily recall or account for what we've done or why we've done it: Where did I put my keys? Why did I burst into tears during that coffee advert? Why did I go to get a screwdriver from that drawer when I moved the drawers around five years ago? Why did I turn down that invitation? The psychotherapist Stephen Wolinsky (1991) refers to these automatic ways of being as 'trance states' – for much of our waking life we simply habitually/robotically repeat behaviours without being consciously aware of our actions.

The unconscious part of our minds houses the billions of residents living in the complex city. Although the mayor has a degree of governance over how these residents live their lives, on a day-to-day basis they function without interference or supervision from the civic leader; they just get on with their work. Unlike the fatigued mayor, the residents have unlimited capacity and capability, working continually – the unconscious mind continues to work even when we're asleep.

One of the functions of the unconscious mind is to maintain the smooth running of our internal bodies and to maximise our physical safety and comfort by altering the functioning of our bodies in response to external stimuli.

Without any awareness on our part, the unconscious mind automatically regulates such things as heart rate, breathing, hormone and chemical release, the immune system, the digestive system and so on. The body is normally kept at an even, comfortable pace. But, when, for example, a threat to the person is detected, the unconscious mind automatically stimulates the fight, flight, freeze (stress) response, preparing the body for physical action – to battle, to run away or to play dead. Adrenalin and cortisol flood the body. The heart rate increases, breathing is quickened, the digestive system is put on hold, and blood is pumped into the limbs. This is an adaptive response that evolved over time to maximise our ability to survive life-threatening situations. But, the unconscious mind lacks the ability to analyse whether the threat it has detected is real or not, and the system can be triggered by perceived dangers that do not actually threaten the survival of the individual; for example, the anticipation of delivering a speech.

As we experience life, the unconscious mind automatically, seemingly flawlessly, develops neural pathways, procedural programmes of 'how to' that generate our everyday physical behaviour. We remain blissfully unaware of all that's going on in the unconscious mind so can slip into autopilot mode and climb a flight of stairs (a massive achievement involving countless neural connections and interactions) whilst consciously counselling a friend; drive from A to B whilst actively planning our next strategic move at work; paint a wall whilst thinking about how to best help our 10 year old tackle their algebra homework. The procedural memories formed in the unconscious mind enable us, as human beings, to preserve limited energy supplies, to multi-task and to leave conscious capacity to attend to life in the here and now.

But, the unconscious mind is not just responsible for helping us to physically navigate our way through life. Even before the conscious mind begins developing (remember, it develops from about the age of 2), just as if it were a sponge, the unconscious mind absorbs information. Every experience we have builds information within the unconscious mind about who we are, how we feel and what we do. Belief systems begin to form. As we continue to grow, we continue to experience, and our belief systems are reinforced and added to. These belief systems become templates in the unconscious mind of 'how to respond' to specific situations, and habitual, automatic behavioural responses form (aka, situation-dependent automatic states of mind).

When Duncan was a child, and he'd hurt himself, or someone had been nasty to him, if she was around, his adoptive grandmother would do her best to make him feel better by giving him a huge hug and something sweet to eat – normally chocolate. He remembers the, albeit fleeting, sense of safety in his grandmother's arms, the warmth of the embrace and the taste and smooth texture of that chocolate. He learned that security and comfort were linked to chocolate. The belief that 'chocolate is a comfort' formed and so did the habitual, comforting behaviour: 'When I need comfort, I eat chocolate'. When Duncan's relationship with his girlfriend Jenny ended, he automatically turned to chocolate for comfort. He put on weight. The more weight he gained, the more unattractive he felt, the more stressed he became, the more comfort he needed, the more chocolate he ate.

After successfully completing her A levels, Mia studied English at University. She worked hard every day to take on board all that she was being taught. Every evening Mia and her friends would drink wine to unwind and relax after their endeavours. Over time, she learned that wine relaxed her and rewarded her for all that grafting. So, in her current role as mother, after a long day with her two children, Mia would habitually head for the fridge and pour herself a very large glass of wine as a reward for making it through the day.

But, we are regularly told by 'those what know' (the experts) that drinking too much alcohol and eating too many sugary foods will damage our health in the long run. Our belief that wine and chocolate are beneficial is, therefore, inaccurate.

This highlights a major flaw of the unconscious mind; it neither challenges nor analyses information received from the external world, but simply absorbs and stores all that it receives. The unconscious mind lacks the ability to distinguish between fact and fantasy so, once the information has been absorbed into the mind, it is accepted as truth, whether it's right or wrong, beneficial or not. The belief that wine and chocolate are constructive becomes a 'fact' in our minds, and this 'fact' then automatically steers our behaviour.

How can we go about changing an inaccurate belief? Surely being told reliable new information is enough to make us change our minds? Strangely, in general, the answer is 'no'. This can be effective, but typically, once these belief systems are formed they are very difficult to consciously change. The reason is that the conscious part of our minds acts as a gate-keeper, an authoritarian civic leader, who filters out information that goes against our established beliefs (beliefs that are housed in the unconscious mind). This filter is known as the *Reticular Activating System* (RAS).

For example, you hold the belief that drinking a lot of beer is good for you because it relaxes you. You have endless experiences of drinking large quantities of beer and feeling relaxed to prove it. When the experts tell you otherwise, the conscious mind analyses the new information, is aware of the conflicting data, and, because your continued experience of drinking lots of beer supports your belief, it filters out the healthier truth in

34

favour of maintaining your own truth. The new information is rejected by the conscious mind and so does not pass through to the unconscious mind where it could take seed, form a new belief and a new pattern of response.

To re-cap: Much as it might be uncomfortable to accept, most of our behaviour is not consciously driven. It is instigated automatically by the unconscious mind that lies beyond our conscious awareness and control. Based on our experiences we form belief systems that inform our habitual responses to specific situations (we develop situation-dependent automatic states of mind). But, these belief systems might not be built on fact, and the consequential behavioural responses might not be, in the long run, the best way of going forward. Once these belief systems and habitual responses are formed, they are difficult to change because they are protected by the conscious mind via the RAS. The conscious mind filters out (rejects) information that is inconsistent with the mind's pre-formed beliefs.

Therefore, because the vast majority of our behaviour is generated by the unconscious mind, to change these patterns of response, we need to switch off the analytical conscious mind and its filter system, and gain direct access to the unconscious mind.

And this is where hypnosis comes in.

In relation to your behaviour, begin to think through your automatic responses to specific situations.

How might your habitual behaviours be impacting your current sense of discomfort and dissatisfaction?

Progress report:

My expectations: You now have a clearer understanding of how your mind is generating your behaviour, and are beginning to become more aware of your own set of automatic/habitual responses to specific situations.

What you've learned:

How this knowledge affects your perception of the discomfort and dissatisfaction that you're currently experiencing:

Chapter 2

What is hypnotherapy?

Before we begin this chapter, write down your current understanding of what hypnotherapy is. Make a note of any worries you have regarding hypnotherapy.

There is neither mystery nor magic to hypnotherapy, but there are many misunderstandings concerning what it is.

Perhaps the most popular misconception of hypnotherapy centres on an all-powerful, sinister hypnotist placing a weak-willed victim into a sleep-like state to gain complete control over them for their own amusement or wicked ends. Given this media-fuelled scenario, the thought of being made to squawk like a chicken on command, or rob a bank, or worse still, typically creates a sense of mistrust and fear, even amongst the most open-minded. It would me.

But the above bears no resemblance to clinical hypnotherapy. Phew!

Clinical hypnotherapy is a safe, non-addictive and, above all, effective form of treatment for many psychological and physical (yes, physical) conditions. The chief aim of hypnotherapy applied within the clinical context is to help people overcome issues that are having a detrimental impact on their life.

You'll all be aware of hypnotherapy being used to help people stop smoking (mentioning some names you'll probably be familiar with: Matt Damon, Ashton Kutcher, Ben Affleck and Drew Barrymore); to lose weight (Lily Allen, Sarah Ferguson, Sophie Dahl and Geri Halliwell); to overcome fears and phobias; to control panic and anxiety; to enhance performance (Tiger Woods, Jimmy Connors, Kevin McBride, Adam Walker, Steve Hooker and Rod Carew). But hypnotherapy is also used to help people combat physical issues and illnesses (for example, Bruce Willis and Julia Roberts saw hypnotherapists to help them overcome stuttering problems).

Please be aware from the outset that I'm not suggesting for one moment that hypnotherapy can provide a remedy for all physical illnesses. No, no and no, again. If a client presents with a physical ailment, I ask them first to visit their GP and then work alongside the GP's diagnosis and choice of medication. But, having said this, hypnotherapy *has* been used to ease a wide range of physical ailments ranging from pain relief to speeding up the process of healing broken bones, to even enabling people to undertake surgery and dental treatment without medical anaesthetic, and so much more. And, of course, every physical illness has psychological consequences that hypnotherapy can help address.

Myth busting

1. There's no hocus pocus, no calling on supernatural forces, no waving of pocket watches; clinical hypnotherapy is an effective process of change that rests on our scientific understanding of how the human mind works. Through the process of hypnosis (the

38

generation of the trance state) the Reticular Activating System of the conscious mind can be by-passed and direct access to the unconscious mind can be achieved.

2. Hypnosis (the trance state), originating from the Greek word 'hypnos' meaning 'sleep', suggests that the trance is a sleep-like state of mind. It is not. In fact, when a human being is asleep, their unconscious mind is fully internally occupied. Given that the hypnotherapist needs the attention of the unconscious mind to generate change, sleep is clearly not desirable. So, should someone inadvertently fall asleep during trance, the hypnotherapist brings them up to a lighter state of relaxation. (Should you fall asleep whilst listening to the hypnosis audios that accompany this book – other than Audio 1: Good night, sleep well – just listen to it again when you're less tired.)

3. People also often voice concerns about not being able to 'wake up' after being in hypnosis, but given that hypnosis is not a sleep state, when the trance comes to an end, the conscious mind returns.

4. It is often thought that hypnosis can make people do things, whether they want to do them or not. This is not so. It is not possible through hypnosis to make anyone do anything that they don't want to do. As a hypnotherapist, I cannot make you do anything you don't want to do.

5. It is frequently believed that only those who are 'very suggestible' or weak can enter a hypnotic trance and

so benefit from hypnosis. Again, this is not the case. Almost everybody can be hypnotised *if they want to be*, apart perhaps from those who are unable to focus their attention for prolonged periods of time, such as the very young or very old, or those who are under the influence of alcohol or drugs.

What is 'hypnosis'?

'Hypnosis' means the trance state. The trance is created to bypass the logical conscious mind and its Reticular Activating System, and gain direct access to the unconscious mind.

The trance is a calm, pleasant feeling, similar to daydreaming, in which the conscious part of the mind is relaxed and the awareness of the unconscious mind heightened. 'It is a mental state in which a person's perceptions and observations flow unobstructed' by pre-set procedural programmes (Stephen Wolinsky, 1991). The brain wave activity during hypnosis slows down to a frequency level called alpha, a state we pass through on the way to and from sleep. Importantly, people remain aware of what is happening to them, and retain absolute free will and self-control at all times.

Relaxation of the conscious mind is actually a naturally occurring state that you will have experienced every day of your life, many times a day – you simply didn't realise it. As you'll remember from the previous chapter, we spend much of our waking lives in various trance (autopilot) states of mind.

Stephen Wolinsky suggests that the human trance state is universally experienced and that 100 per cent of the world's population experience it on a daily basis (2007).

In fact, we dip in and out of trance states every day, at times in which we're physically present but consciously absent. For example, you will feel it nightly just before you fall asleep or when you're daydreaming or absorbed in a book or film, or even when you're driving – so-called 'highway hypnosis'. The reason television advertising is so powerful is because watching TV typically relaxes the body which, in itself, induces a trance-like state. Therefore, many of the advertising messages to buy something slip through the RAS of the conscious mind and lodge in the unconscious, creating a demand and a desire for a product that you didn't have before. Ah, yes – that explains why I went off-piste and felt impelled to buy that room freshener!

How do you hypnotise someone?

As far as I'm concerned, there are three stages to the hypnotherapeutic process – induction, re-programming and emergence.

Induction

There are many ways to help a person enter trance – it's called the induction process – but none of these is effective if that person insists that they will not be hypnotised. My preferred method of induction, the technique I use with most of my clients and the approach I use in the audios that accompany this book, centres on encouraging the Reticular Activating System of the conscious mind to slip away through simple relaxation of the physical body. This is referred to as a Permissive/Progressive Relaxation Induction, using language that invites the body to let go. Such an induction is not only effective, it's also thoroughly enjoyable and incredibly beneficial to both the body and the mind.

Relaxation is physically restorative. It boosts the body's immune system, lowers blood pressure, allows the muscle cells to strengthen and re-build, and the organs of the body to function optimally. And, relaxation benefits us psychologically too. It re-balances the mind and the body, calming the mind, allowing us to see things in their true perspective, to tune into our knowledge base and find the solutions to our life issues. Relaxation has also been shown to reduce psychological conditions such as depression and anxiety.

To give a little more detail of how you will be eased into the trance state, each audio will ask you to find a comfortable, warm and safe place in which to lie back and begin relaxing. Neutral music will play in the background of the audio. When a person is experiencing a psychological or physical problem, their breathing can become very shallow and/or overly fast, so, each recording begins with an exercise to deepen and slow the breathing – the 5/7 breathing. The breathing exercise is very straight forward. It simply involves inhaling slowly for the count of 5, allowing the stomach to rise with each inhalation, and then exhaling for the count of 7, allowing the stomach to fall with each outward breath. My voice will then guide you through a gentle and pleasurable process of physical and mental relaxation. Following the induction process, the focus of each session will then gently unfold.

Remember, I cannot *force* you to relax – I invite you to do so; you will enter the trance state when you *allow* yourself physically to let go.

Re-programming: Hypnotherapeutic methods of change

Once the trance state is achieved, there are many varied and creative methods available to the hypnotherapist to facilitate positive re-programming of the unconscious mind. Should you be interested in learning about these and other methods in more depth, I recommend you investigate the references at the end of this chapter because, in an attempt to keep 'on point', I will only (and briefly) describe the methods that are specifically relevant to this book.

1. Direct Positive Suggestion

Direct Positive Suggestion is one of the most straightforward, therapist-directed methods employed by hypnotherapists to enable change. Based on pre-discussed goals, new information that will override old dysfunctional beliefs and behavioural responses is put forward to an individual whilst they are in the trance state. Because the conscious mind is switched off, these messages get through to the unconscious mind to form new neural pathways that inform more beneficial beliefs, thoughts, feelings, physiological responses and behaviours.

2. Parts therapy

Parts therapy is an empowering technique to help people identify their own solutions to specific issues. It is based on two specific concepts: that each person has the resources within them to solve their own problems, and that human beings are comprised of many different parts or sub-personalities, each with different drives and abilities.

Within our everyday lives, we perform many

different roles, each role requiring specific capabilities and skill-sets to best function within that role. For much of the time, these parts operate in harmony with each other, each part coming to the fore at the appropriate time. For example, in our work role, the part of us that is organised, goal-directed and assertive will perhaps be dominant, and, when we're out with our friends, the part of us that is fun and sociable might take the lead. But, there are times when these parts are at odds with each other generating conflicting feelings and behaviours. Let's say that someone wants to become a non-smoker, yet they keep buying cigarettes. Here, the part of the person that focuses on health and well-being is in conflict with the part that defines itself as 'smoker'. Parts therapy provides the opportunity to mediate between these opposing parts to resolve the conflict.

Sometimes we experience uncomfortable feelings yet find it difficult to put our finger on quite what it is we're feeling and what might be causing those feelings (feelings of discomfort perhaps). This is where parts therapy can come into its own – it can be applied as a 'bottom-up' diagnostic tool. It enables a person to examine their discomfort in detail and to become more familiar with how it's represented in their body and mind. By understanding how the discomfort feels in the body, where it's located, how it looks and sounds, insights can be gained into what it is and what might be causing and/or maintaining it.

3. Visualisation

Experiencing discomfort and dissatisfaction can lead us to avoid the emotion-driving situations. But, avoiding the things that trigger the discomfort simply serves to perpetuate it. It stands to reason therefore, that exposure to the stimulus, gaining more comfortable experience, will be beneficial. But, the thought of exposure to something that we find uncomfortable can feel very challenging.

Visualisation offers us the opportunity to gain positive experience of the taxing situation in a completely safe and supportive environment. This is how: Neuro-imaging techniques have demonstrated that when we visualise doing something, our neurons fire as though we were really doing it. As far as our unconscious minds are concerned, what's imagined is real and that information is then stored as factual. The more richly we imagine something, the more vibrantly it will be remembered, and the more powerful its effect will be in informing future behaviour. Thus, to gain positive experience of the challenging stimulus, all we need do is visualise it.

Visualisations can be therapist directed or the individual can be encouraged to visualise freely. Adam Walker, the first British man to swim the toughest seven oceans of the world, uses visualisation techniques whilst swimming to help him manage the cold of the water. He visualises the warmth of a bath, and imagines that warmth to such effect that his brain accepts that his body is warm and comfortable and so allows him to continue swimming despite the cold.

4. Pseudo-orientation in time

When people are experiencing difficulties, the future can often seem very bleak. But, within trance, by orientating the mind into the future, a person can be enabled to visualise a desired state of being as though that state had already been achieved. As with visualisation, the mind then accepts what has been imagined as though it were real and inevitable, and so automatically guides that person toward making this their reality.

5. Anchoring

Installing an anchor is a quick and effective method of enabling someone to enter a resourceful/beneficial state of mind on demand. Anchoring is a technique that overrides past detrimental responses to specific situations and provides a person with a sense of confidence in their ability to control how they choose to respond to something.

Anchoring without trance is an NLP (Neuro-linguistic Programming) technique that aims to override past detrimental responses (fear for example) to a specific stimulus (a spider), and put in place a consistent, healthy learned response to that stimulus (calm interest). But, my work has taught me that anchors set within the trance state (without the interference of logic) are even more powerful and enduring. The theoretical basis for anchoring lies within Classical Conditioning, learning through association. (For a more thorough explanation of Anchoring and Classical Conditioning, see Chapter 6.)

An anchor can typically take the form of a word or phrase, an image, a smell, a number or a physical action but can be represented by anything to do with our five senses. My preferred anchor is the gentle pressing together of the thumb and index finger of the dominant hand.

6. Regression

We learn from our past experiences, and some of those lessons are highly beneficial to us, reinforcing a positive sense of who we are and what we're capable of.

Regression has many uses, but it is a hypnotherapeutic method chiefly applied to investigate and heal past unresolved experiences that are negatively affecting a person's present life. Ideally it looks to resolve issues surrounding the initial event that first triggered the negative response, the Initial Sensitising Event.

It rests on the understanding that the unconscious mind stores memories of everything we've ever experienced (whether we can actively remember those experiences or not), memories that automatically inform and reinforce our belief systems, thoughts, feelings and behaviours. Whilst in a safe and relaxed trance state, these memories are encouraged to come forward to be modified through:

- Dissociation (disconnecting the person from the experience, not only protecting them from possible further discomfort generated by remembering the event, but also facilitating lessons to be learned through observation of it)
- De-sensitisation (diminishing uncomfortable emotional states attached to the event)
- Re-framing (establishing new interpretations and meanings of the event).

Please be aware that it is possible during Regression for once-repressed memories to emerge, memories that were hidden by the unconscious mind due to the troubling nature of the experience. Should this happen, although uncomfortable at the time, see it as a highly positive step forward, a sign that your unconscious mind is now ready to begin dealing with difficult past issues, and, as soon as you're able to do so, make an appointment to see a qualified clinical hypnotherapist to help you work it through.

7. Chair Therapy

There are multiple ways in which Chair Therapy can be used and adapted within hypnotherapy, but, in general, Chair Therapy facilitates a sense of closure and healing. It encourages someone to imagine themselves in a very safe and secure room, sitting comfortably in a chair, facing a seated person from their past or present, a person whom, perhaps, they did not get the chance to say 'goodbye' to, a person who hurt them, or a person whom they hurt.

It is vital within Chair Therapy for each individual to know that they are the one who is in control of events that unfold, so, as I apply it, there are three primary directives within the process:

- The other person may only enter the room when invited to do so
- They must leave the room when asked
- They may not respond to what is being said unless invited to.

Depending on the nature of the issue in hand, the individual is given the opportunity to talk to the other person in the room with them, to get off their chest/release all they want to say where this other is concerned. It's cathartic.

Chair Therapy can also be used to mentally rehearse future conversations/situations.

Emergence

The final stage of the hypnotherapeutic process is to bring a person back to full awareness – emergence. I do this by counting from 3 up to 1, with each count encouraging the individual to become more alert and more aware until, at the count of 1, I ask for their eyes to open and the conscious mind to fully re-engage.

Note that within each hypnosis session, you may experience a degree of time distortion, with time seeming to shrink or expand, and you may not have a complete memory of all that transpired during the session. Please do not worry about either of these things. If time seems to have slowed down or speeded up, it simply demonstrates that you were in a trance state. And, if you can't consciously recall all that happened, fear not – your unconscious mind will have a complete memory of what was said and what was achieved, and will begin authomatically to act on what was learned.

To re-cap: Clinical hypnotherapy is a safe and enduringly effective client-centred therapy, its chief goal being to help people overcome issues that are having a detrimental effect on their life. Based on our understanding that the majority of what human beings do, think and feel is automatically driven by the unconscious mind, clinical hypnotherapy uses hypnosis (the trance state) to by-pass the RAS of the conscious mind and gain direct access to the unconscious mind. Once access to the unconscious mind has been achieved, various methods are applied to generate positive, lasting change.

Progress report:

My expectations: You now have a clearer understanding of what hypnotherapy is and how clinical hypnotherapists can use hypnosis (the trance state) to generate change.

What you've learned:

How this knowledge affects your perception of the discomfort and dissatisfaction you're currently experiencing:

Further reading suggestions

Elman, D., *Hypnotherapy* (Westwood Publishing Co, new edition, 1984)

Erickson, M. H., *My Voice Will Go With You: Teaching Tales of Milton H. Erickson*, Sydney Rosen (ed.) (W.W. Norton and Company, 1991)

Hadley, J. and Staudacher, C., *Hypnosis for Change* (New Harbinger Publications, 1996)

Hunter, R., *The Art of Hypnotherapy* (Crown House Publishing, 2010)

James, T., with Flores, L. and Schober, J., *Hypnosis – A Comprehensive Guide – Producing Deep Trance Phenomena* (Crown House Publishing Ltd, 2000)

Silvester, T., *Cognitive Hypnotherapy: What's That About and How Can I Use It? Two Simple Questions for Change* (Matador 2010)

Wolinsky, S., *Trances People Live: Healing Approaches in Quantum Psychology* (Bramble Books, 2007)

Chapter 3

Identifying barriers to change

You're uncomfortable about something in your life, feeling ineffective, unsettled and dissatisfied. You'd benefit from making changes. But, does change feel possible for you? Do you perhaps find yourself making excuses where change is concerned?

This chapter focuses on attitudes of mind that could sabotage your efforts to generate change, attitudes such as, 'I can't change'; 'I was born this way'; 'I'm powerless to change'; 'I'm afraid of change'; 'I'll make mistakes and fail'; 'I can't be bothered to change'.

Change, as defined by the Oxford English Dictionary, means 'to become different' or 'to make different'. With these definitions in mind, I now introduce you to six attitudinal barriers to change:

1. How can I become different when I was born the way I am?

When it comes to the concept of 'becoming different', one of the most common concerns voiced by new clients is 'I am the way I am. I was born this way. I can't change'.

But, are these statements true? Is it the genes that we're born with that dictate who we are and how we behave or rather, the experiences we have in the environment in which we're raised, that teach us who to be and how to behave? Yes, that old nugget: The nature/nurture debate.

It is certainly true that many animals are born genetically pre-programmed to behave in specific ways – a salmon returning to its place of birth to spawn for example, a bird's migration to warmer climes, and so on. Yet, for human beings it is different.

You may believe that you were born the way you are, Duncan certainly did, yet, when you really think about it, from the moment you were born, you have changed on a daily basis, some changes being more radical than others. You were born with certain hardwired abilities to cry, to suckle, to turn your head toward the source of potential food, but you had to learn how to hold your head unaided, how to sit, to crawl, to toddle, to walk, to run, to eat, to gabble, to talk, to sing, to debate and so on. You have already learned to accommodate so much change, but it felt so natural, you didn't acknowledge it as change.

We are born into this world with a brain full of billions of neurons, some hardwired abilities, some genetic predispositions and a whole lot of potential. This potential is fashioned by the environment we live in, the experiences we have and the resulting neural pathways that are formed and strengthened.

In his latest book *Not in Your Genes* (2016), Oliver James says 'there is a mass of solid evidence that how we are nurtured makes an enormous difference to how we turn out, for good and ill'. Based on the findings obtained through analysis of the Human Genome Project (2000), it has been demonstrated that individual genes for *psychological traits* of any kind do not exist, and that genes explain only 1-5 per cent of the variation of human mental abilities and personalities. It has been concluded that it is the environment in which we grow and experience life that generates who we become. Who we are is learned and, therefore, can be changed if so desired. We are not fixed in set cement. Yeah!

Our genes may at some level pre-dispose us toward certain physical characteristics, but our brains need experience to form neural connections. If neural pathways are not utilised, the potential abilities they offer tend to fade and die – neurons that fire together, wire together; neurons that fire apart, depart. For instance, we may be born with the ability of sight, but if we're not exposed to 'normal' visual stimuli, the neural pathways that are devoted to sight will not be stimulated and will, because of lack of use, become defunct. This was demonstrated via experiments on new-born kittens in 1963 (Hubel and Wiesel). They found that if a kitten was deprived of normal visual experience during that critical period at the start of its life, the circuitry of the neurons in its visual cortex was irreversibly altered. Another example: we may be born with the potential to be tall (both of our parents are tall), but, if we're born into an impoverished environment in which we're regularly malnourished, we might never reach our height potential.

In *The Brain* (2015), David Eagleman, an

American neuroscientist who specialises in the plasticity (malleability) of the brain, states that genes give a very general direction of how neural paths in the brain may form and function but that 'world experience fine-tunes the rest of the wiring, allowing the human to adapt to the local details of their surroundings'. He continues, 'The human brain is born unfinished and allows itself to be shaped by the details of life experiences.' For example, in 2006, another neuroscientist, James Fallon, inadvertently discovered that he had 'the brain imaging pattern and genetic makeup of a full-blown psychopath'. However, having been born into a nurturing and loving environment, although he did lack empathy, rather than commit heinous crimes, he became a 'successful scientist and family man'. As he surmises, 'I never knew how profoundly an (early) environment could affect somebody'.

A child's brain rapidly develops until the age of about 2, but the process of building a human brain takes up to 25 years. Even when full development of the brain has been achieved, it continues to change through experience. 'Your family of origin, your culture, your friends, your work, every conversation you've ever had – all these have left their footprints in your nervous system. Everything contributes to a continual reshaping of the neural networks we summarize as us' (Eagleman, 2015).

Every day of our lives, with every experience that we have, we have changed and adapted to our environment. From birth to death, we are works in progress. We *are* capable of changing. We do change. FACT.

Having read the above, do you believe that you are capable of changing?

From birth to date, list some of the ways in which you have changed.

2. **How can I make things different when I am powerless to change?**
Have you picked up this book, I wonder, in the hope that I will resolve your problem for you?

It's true that I do sincerely want this book to be of use to you. And, I would, in some ways, love to have the abilities to resolve all people's problems. If this were the case, I would become very powerful indeed ('SuperChris', methinks) for each person who looked to me to resolve their problem on their behalf, would, in fact, be giving away their power to me.

Let me explain further:

You're feeling ineffective within yourself or uncomfortable about something in your life. You want things to be different. But, how did your life get to this point? Do you firmly believe that you and your current situation are simply a product of your circumstances? Do you feel you are where you are because you've been driven by others' dictates, their 'musts', 'shoulds' and 'oughts'? Do you believe that the direction your life has taken has been determined by forces that lie beyond your control? Destiny? Luck? Bad luck? If so, you will probably have formed the belief that you are not in control of your own life and that you have no power to bring about change.

This view of life represents a responsibility-avoidance mind-set, because if you negate any sense of power and control, then nothing is your fault. If this is the case for you, you are living 'at effect'.

Difficult things do happen from time to time; it's part of being alive. But, living 'at effect' means routinely having things happen *to* you, habitually looking outside of yourself for someone/something to blame for how you feel, for what's happened or for what you've not achieved. People who live 'at effect' typically experience feelings of loss of control, fear, anxiety, powerlessness, dependency and hopelessness, remaining, on an everyday basis, passively within the confines of their comfort zone. This is where Mia and Duncan found themselves to be.

Living with the 'at effect' mind-set you believe 'I can't', and simply hope that things will change or that others will make things better for you. You make yourself a victim of circumstance. And, when you believe yourself to be helpless in a situation, you automatically filter out all the possible ways in which you could take control and create something different, because you simply don't see that there are alternative opportunities. Thus, in your own mind, the belief that 'you can't' becomes true.

As young children, we tend to be offered very little control over our own lives, for good reason – we don't know what we're doing. But, as we grow, we experiment and develop, and ideally learn ways in which we take up the reins and become responsible for the direction our own life takes. We learn to develop an 'at cause' mind-set. Within this approach, we believe ourselves to be the creator of our lives, accepting responsibility for who we are and who we will become, the choices we make and the consequences that will result.

Being 'at cause' is approaching life from the position of having personal power and authority over what happens and how we choose to feel about it. It's about actively taking control.

Central to living 'at cause' is the belief 'I can'. We are motivated to look at ourselves and to understand how we can start to do things differently. We believe ourselves to be the creator of what happens in our lives, learning from any mistakes made, taking self-responsibility, and choosing our own end result.

Throughout our daily lives, there will be aspects over which we feel particularly in control, and others over which we feel we have little or no authority; depending on what we're doing, we can feel responsible for the outcome, or at the whim of others' behaviour. For example, in our professional role, we might find it pretty straightforward to make decisions. But, when it comes to our domestic lives, we might leave decision-making to our partner.

Think through where you are on this spectrum of being 'at cause' or 'at effect' and in what circumstances you become particularly aware of your sense of control or lack of it. What are the typical consequences of your approach in these situations?

If nothing else, what I have learned from working alongside my clients over the years is that the most enduring and successful outcomes result from the individual's acceptance of self-responsibility for creating change and resolving problems.

It is my role, as therapist, to provide information and to ask questions that help people understand their problem in more detail. But, my aim is not to tell them what's right for them to do; there are no rights and wrongs, just choices with consequences. I will direct you through the process of change and enable you to see the resources you have to equip you to change, but it is down to you to put the work in, to take action and to make the changes.

There have, sadly, been a few occasions when I have been unsuccessful with a client. Typically this lack of success has centered on the client's misconception that hypnotherapy can *make* a person change, whether they want to or not. As you will have read in Chapter 2, this is not possible. I cannot make anyone do anything they don't want to do. It is for the person desiring change to acknowledge that change will only occur when they take personal responsibility for that change.

Let me explain through example. A couple of years ago, a client came to me presenting with weight problems. There were no medical reasons to explain why she was overweight. She was adamant that she did not over-eat and couldn't understand why she had put on weight; she felt despondent. She didn't recognise the part she had played in the problem arising and felt at the mercy of the weight she had gained. Because she took no responsibility for her weight problem, she saw no need to change her behaviour. She had heard that hypnotherapy was like magic – that it could, in one or two sessions, make anyone do anything, even if they didn't want to do it. She wanted me to make her thin whilst she continued to eat as before. Alas, she was disappointed.

Think of a successful person you know and admire. To what do you attribute their success? Were they just lucky, were they born a genius, or did they simply work hard?

How have you tackled past problems? Have you overcome things that you didn't think you could? If so, take an example of one that you're proud of and reflect on how you achieved it.

Reflect a moment on all that you have achieved to date, no matter how trivial you think the achievement is, and make a list of these achievements.

Where your own sense of discomfort is concerned, reflect on whether you're waiting for things to change or investigating ways in which you can make things change. What, if anything, is stopping you from changing?

3. **How can I make things different when I'm afraid of change?**
Some people thrive on change and enjoy the thrill of the unknown. For others, change can feel big and

frightening; it suggests a state of huge uncertainty and can stop them taking action. Fear of change can call into question our confidence in the resources and abilities that we have, generating self-defeating doubts. And, these doubts automatically trigger the fight/flight/freeze (stress) response, creating that physical discomfort.

But, the fact is that fear, although physically uncomfortable to experience, is nothing more than an emotional response to a *perceived* threat. We perceive change to be a threat; and yet, as already discussed, we continue to change on a daily basis, adapting to what's around us. Some changes are bigger than others, for example getting divorced or being bereaved, but change, whether small or large, is a very normal part of our lives and we are fundamentally adept at accommodating it. It may challenge us, but key to managing change is our belief that we have the skills and abilities, the resources, to rise to it and the knowledge that we will handle it.

Change can also feel rather frightening to those immediately around us. When we change or are changing, others can find it difficult to accept and might consciously (or unconsciously) look for ways to keep us as we were. Perhaps a jealous husband prefers their partner to remain overweight for fear of losing them should their goal be achieved. They might then buy chocolates, suggest going out for dinners and so on to sabotage their efforts to lose weight. The friend of a person wishing to stop smoking might fear losing that friend, so encourage the person to remain a smoker; or, they may feel even worse about their own smoking habit should their friend quit, so, again, encourage the friend to remain a smoker. These forms of sabotage are rarely deliberately undertaken, but they can play a key role in a person's ability to achieve their goal.

Mia's husband, Geoff, found the changes that she made led to his needs no longer being prioritised as they once had been. He remonstrated and accused in an attempt to maintain the status quo. She learned to acknowledge his fears where she was concerned and enabled him to talk through his uneasiness. By discussing her goals with him and keeping him 'in the loop' on a regular basis, she was able to help him realise that, in the long run, he would benefit too.

In what circumstances do you fear change?

Hold that fear up to the light and examine it; what does it mean to you?

What skills and abilities do you have that will enable you to accommodate change?

How might your changing affect others around you?

4. **How can I make things different when I'm convinced I'll make mistakes and that I'll fail?**

   All human beings are fallible – we make mistakes and we all fail at things from time to time. Yet, rather than accept this as a normal part of life, we can grow up terrified of getting things wrong and almost phobic of the shame that failing can generate.

Mia was one of these people. When her parents' marriage began to degenerate, their tolerance for mistakes plummeted; they didn't have the energy reserves to view Mia's errors, or her siblings' or each other's errors as anything other than a burden. Mia was regularly scolded for things that she got wrong and, as time went by, she developed a fear of making mistakes. In her attempt to minimise the likelihood of her making mistakes, she began setting incredibly high standards for herself. But, far from reducing her chances of making a mistake, this approach resulted in her feeling a sense of almost permanent failure.

Her parents became so self-focused that they were unable to help Mia differentiate between her behaviour and her value as a human being, and she began to view her mistakes and failures as a reflection of her ineptitude and worthlessness. Her self-esteem plummeted and she strived even harder at school, driven to get the best grades that she could to please her troubled parents and make them proud of her.

The fear of making mistakes and failing can often lead us to form unconsciously driven self-sabotage behaviours that set us against achieving our goal and so maintain the problematic behaviour. These sabotage behaviours include procrastination, putting things off until conditions are met that will 'guarantee' success; perfectionism, setting unattainably high standards for self (as in the case of Mia) and avoidance, side-stepping a situation to hide flaws from others and avoid risking public shame (as in the case of Duncan).

But, evidence demonstrates that it is the most successful people in society who make the most mistakes and live through the most failures. Making mistakes and not succeeding at things is an invaluable part of realising how to (or how not to) do something. Based on the lessons learned, we adapt our behaviour to better effect; we adjust what we're doing and how we're doing it. Thomas Edison found many ways of not making an electric light bulb before he finally found out how to make one. 'I have not failed,' he said, 'I've just found 10,000 ways that won't work'.

To further explain this, let's look at learning a new skill – playing rugby. Perhaps it was different for Owen Farrell, 2016 Six Nations England fly half, I don't know, but for most of us, the first time we find ourselves on a rugby playing field, we don't have much idea of what to do or how to do it. There are rules a-plenty. We need to be taught how to pass the ball, to kick the ball, the role each team member plays in the game, etc. There's a host of information and new skills to take on board. At first we might apply our foot to the ball intending it to fly into the air in one direction, and find that it's heading in quite the opposite way. We learn that the error happened because we had placed our foot on the wrong part of the ball. So we learn to kick more effectively and we practise and we practise and we practise, until gradually we learn what's necessary to play rugby effectively. We know that Farrell, from time to time, misses penalty kicks – he is human.

How do you define a 'mistake' and a 'failure'?

Identify some of your past mistakes and failures.

What were the consequences of these?

Having made these mistakes and lived through these failures, what lessons did you learn? How did you grow as a person?

With your definitions of a 'mistake' and a 'failure' in mind, are these definitions helpful to you in any way? If not, what would be a more beneficial way of viewing mistakes and failures?

Would you describe yourself as a perfectionist? If so, in what circumstances do you find yourself being more perfectionist than others? What are the typical consequences of you being perfectionist in these circumstances?

Do you tend to put things off? If so, under what circumstances do you do this? Again, what are the typical consequences of procrastinating in these situations?

Do you tend to avoid things? If so, what type of things do you routinely avoid and with what consequences?

5. But, if I change, I might have to give up ... secondary gains

Difficult though it may be to identify and acknowledge, for every long-term problem experienced, there will be some, albeit perhaps subtle, benefits derived from the issue continuing – this is what we call secondary gains.

For example, the problem we have might be acting as a shield, as an excuse to avoid doing certain things that we don't want to do; the problem might provide us with a lot of attention from other people, attention that we enjoy; the problem might act as an excuse for maintaining behaviours such as drinking too much, overeating, smoking and so on, behaviours that we want to continue doing.

Due to her experiences, Mia lacked belief in her ability to make wise decisions. Whenever she could, she avoided making decisions. In so doing she felt no sense of responsibility for the decisions that others made on her behalf – negating responsibility was Mia's secondary gain.

Without necessarily being consciously aware of them, these secondary gains might be so useful to us that they generate self-sabotaging behaviours where our efforts to create change are concerned.

Mia felt so troubled by the prospect of learning how to take responsibility that she cancelled an appointment with me.

With secondary gains in mind, is your sense of discomfort beneficial to you in any way?

6. **How can I make things different when I am not committed to doing so?**

We've discussed some of the attitudinal obstacles faced when considering the prospect of change. But, change is made even more difficult when we're neither fully motivated nor 100% committed to making it happen.

Motivation is, simply put, the desire to do something. We all experience motivation at some levels: unless we're naturists, we typically get dressed before we leave our home; we brush our teeth and wash ourselves; we eat and drink. But, finding the motivation to change can feel more difficult, more challenging.

In order to help ourselves to develop a sense of motivation toward our goal, it's important to acknowledge all the rewards that we'll enjoy as a result of achieving it. By understanding how we'll benefit from our goal, we can begin to fully realise that it is something we really want, something, therefore, to get excited about; something that warrants our effort. Motivation gives us the confidence to step out of our comfort zones, face any difficulties that arise, and achieve. Rather than 'because I ought to', 'I should' or 'I have to', 'because I *want* to' is the language of the motivated.

And, related to this is commitment. The 'I'll try' or 'I'll give it a go' approach simply won't cut it; it suggests a half-hearted attitude that, particularly at times of strain, is easily defeated. One of the ways in which commitment can be generated is by understanding how the proposed change fits into the bigger picture of our lives. Change for change's sake, or change that will not enhance our lives in the long run seems futile, not worth the effort, nigh on impossible to commit to. Yet, when we can see the value of the change in relation to improving our lives as a whole, we are more likely to commit ourselves to achieving it, and so dramatically increase our chances of successful change. 'I will' and 'I am' is the language of the committed.

We will address these issues in more detail in the following chapter when we begin identifying the specifics of your goal.

Progress report:

My expectations: you now have an understanding that people can and do change. It stands to reason, therefore, that you can change.

Furthermore:

- You are now willing to accept full responsibility for making change happen.
- You are aware that you have the resources to handle change.
- You are aware that change can challenge those near and dear to you.
- You acknowledge that it's OK to make mistakes – that you can learn from them.
- You have identified any secondary gains that you might be experiencing.

- You know how change will fit into the bigger picture of your life and feel motivated and committed to making changes.

What you've learned:

How this knowledge affects your perception of your current discomfort and dissatisfaction:

Chapter 4

The first step of the change process – understanding what is

Investigating your presenting issue and designing your goal

The first step of the change process is to gain a thorough understanding of the problem as it stands. This is often not nearly as straightforward as you think it's going to be; a person's presenting issue is so often muddled by all sorts of past and present interconnecting issues. I regularly refer to such situations as being like a ball of tangled threads – from a single glance, who knows where one thread begins and another ends? But, it *is* possible to begin to make sense of this morass. The following questions are designed to help you gently tease out one thread from another, highlighting the issues that are problematic to you.

So, we now begin the process of uncovering what your sense of discomfort is and how it's affecting your current life.

What is it about you or your life that you're uncomfortable/dissatisfied with?

For some, this will be relatively easy to identify and describe; for others, it will feel like explaining quantum physics. At this stage, just do your best. (We'll explore the discomfort in far more detail in Chapter 5.)

For how long have you been feeling this sense of discomfort?

In order to gauge your progress, on a scale of 1-10 with 1 being hardly at all and 10 being very, how much of a problem is this for you?

If we're experiencing a problem, we can often begin to define ourselves by it. Once such a self-definition has formed, it can become fixed in our minds as a fact.

Do you define yourself as a person who is dissatisfied and ineffective, or as a person who is currently experiencing these problems?

Is this a constant issue for you or are there times when you are more aware of it being a problem than others?

The *causes* of Mia and Duncan's discomfort were firmly rooted in their pasts, but if the dissatisfaction you're currently feeling is relatively new to you:

Are there any current life issues that are *causing* your discomfort?

There were 4 major issues in Mia's current life that added to her feeling of discomfort.

Current trigger 1: Despite her ambition to become an English teacher, Mia, aged 20, became a mother and, by the age of 22 was a full-time mother of two children. At the time of seeing me her daughters were aged 10 and 8. Both children attended school and participated in many out-of-school activities, activities that were a car journey away from home. Mia was tired and felt stretched to her limits, focusing her attention and energy on satisfying her children's needs.

Current trigger 2: Mia was married to Geoff, the father of their two children, whom she had met at University. Geoff was the sole breadwinner. Mia described him as having traditional expectations of a wife concerning sex, economic frugality, provision of childcare, domestic duties, and so on. He had a tendency to sulk and, if things in the house weren't as he wanted them to be, he became angry and verbally lashed out, his attacks centring on her failure as a person for not meeting his expectations. Despite being quite liberal with what he bought for himself, he kept a tight hold on the purse strings where Mia was concerned. Mia had no financial independence and was expected to ask for money for groceries, etc. She felt guilty spending money on herself. Mia did not confront Geoff but continued to try to fulfil his expectations.

Current trigger 3: Mia's father would phone every other week or so and would spend the time talking about himself and his (new) wife, asking nothing about Mia's welfare.

Current trigger 4: Before marrying Geoff and having two children, Mia had been an independent, ambitious young woman. She routinely felt a sense of disappointment and failure.

And Duncan? What's currently happening in Duncan's life that's contributing to his sense of discomfort?

Current trigger 1: Jenny, Duncan's girlfriend had recently left him. She had retained the communal flat and most of their shared friends, leaving him feeling completely alone. Much against his better judgement, and for want of somewhere to live, Duncan had moved back into his parents' home.

Current trigger 2: Duncan worked for a large, impersonal organisation as an IT specialist. There was a culture within the organisation to view the IT staff as a species apart from the rest of the workforce. The organisation was lax when it came to staff appraisals, recognition of success and positive feedback.

Current trigger 3: Duncan really disliked his appearance and felt unattractive to others.

If you can, identify the specific current things/events/ people/situations (the current triggers) that generate a sense of discomfort and dissatisfaction within you.

Mia's sense of discomfort had many consequences on her life. Emotionally she felt powerless and worthless, physically she suffered from headaches and shoulder pain, she had digestive problems and felt constantly tired, her thoughts centring on self-doubt and self-criticism. She found herself avoiding making decisions, avoiding confrontation, allowing the children's poor behaviour to continue unchecked, and setting ridiculously high standards for herself, standards that she daily failed to meet.

Duncan's sense of discomfort also took its toll on him. He too felt worthless and described himself as 'a waste of space'; he experienced sleep difficulties, waking up many times during the night, starting each new day exhausted. The sheer effort of pretending to be okay also took its toll on him. He felt fraudulent, he felt angry and stressed, his body tense, his stomach nauseous. His thoughts became vengeful at the injustice of it all; he needed others' approval and felt dependent on their favourable judgement of him.

Where this sense of dissatisfaction and discomfort is concerned, what emotional symptoms are you experiencing?

What are your physical symptoms?

What thoughts tend to flow through your mind when you're feeling dissatisfied and uncomfortable?

And, how does the discomfort influence your day-to-day behaviour?

Mia's inability to confront things not only gave indirect permission to her children to misbehave, it also gave her husband a lot of power. Despite loving them, she found herself resenting her husband and children. Geoff's respect for Mia seemed to lessen daily. She felt too tired and too guilty to see friends or to partake in leisure activities, and her life became completely focused on her home.

Duncan was very needy where his girlfriend was concerned and his dependency on her to validate his existence led to the ending of their relationship. The tiredness affected Duncan's ability to work effectively and, rather than receiving the positive feedback that he craved, he was regularly reprimanded by his line manager for underperforming. He spent a fortune on clothes, clothes that he hoped might make him more attractive to others, and he often ended up in debt at the end of the month.

What impact is your discomfort having on the rest of your life, your ability to sleep and eat, your libido, your work, your friendships, your

relationships with significant others, your leisure time, your exercise and so on?

As you might remember, Mia turned to drinking wine to reward herself for managing to endure another day, and Duncan chose chocolate to comfort him.

Do you find yourself reliant on anything to help cope with this discomfort? If so, what might be the long-term implications of continuing this way?

Caffeine, alcohol, drugs, smoking, over-work, physical inactivity, lack of sleep are all known to exacerbate feelings of discomfort.

Are you doing anything that could, inadvertently, be making the problem worse? If so, are you willing to change any of these habits? How will you go about making these changes?

Time and time again, laughter has been shown to be of great therapeutic value; it decreases stress hormones and triggers the release of feel-good endorphins. Laughter promotes an overall sense of well-being and can even relieve the sensations of pain.

What makes you laugh? Do you feel you laugh enough? If not, how could you bring more laughter into your life?

You now know how the sense of discomfort is affecting you in the present. This leads us nicely onto:

How would you prefer to feel? What is your goal state?

Bearing in mind that if we don't know where we're going, we'll probably never get there, establishing goals is an essential part of the change process. Goals give our lives direction and our efforts a focus.

As defined by the Oxford English dictionary, a goal is 'the object of a person's ambition or effort; an aim or desired result', a desired result that a person envisions, plans and commits to achieving.

Goal setting involves the development of an action plan designed to motivate and guide us toward our goal. There are several criteria involved in goal setting. Ideally, we benefit from the goal being:

- **Specific** – by detailing clearly and unambiguously what we want to accomplish, why we want to accomplish it (our motivations and likely rewards) and how we're going to accomplish it (our strategy), we know precisely what to expect and where to focus our energy.
- **Stated in positive terms** – because using positive language tends to reduce conflict and boost motivation, wording our goal as 'to become fit' rather than 'to feel less unhealthy' is of far greater value to us.
- **Attainable** – making sure our goal is realistic is crucial; for example, if we've just been promoted at work or have recently given birth, setting a goal to

walk the Great Wall of China in the next month would probably lead to disappointment.

- **Relevant** – understanding how the goal fits into the bigger picture of our lives facilitates greater commitment to it.
- **Measurable** – when progress is measured, we're more likely to stay on target, so, understanding how we're going to assess our progress helps us keep on course.
- **Time-bound** – setting ourselves a time-frame for completing the goal makes success all the more probable.

Let's look at Mia and Duncan's goals:

Mia was fed up with being a shadow of her former self and wanted to change this. Her goal was to re-find her ambitious, self-directed, self-respecting self, the woman she had been aged 20, just before she became pregnant and dropped out of University. She was motivated by the thought of generating a more equal relationship with Geoff, learning how to confront things within the relationship more successfully, and by the thought of fostering a more loving, more parental role with her daughters in which she felt able to reprimand them when needed. The potential rewards were evident to Mia: She would be able to enjoy life again; to respect herself and earn the respect of her husband and children; to create interest and satisfaction for herself outside the home.

In the longer term, Mia wanted to be able to go back to college to complete her English degree with a view to becoming a teacher, a role she hoped to combine with her current responsibilities.

Based on her goal, I devised a treatment programme for Mia that was to include 11 face-to-face hypnotherapy sessions over a three-month period.

All these rewards were very important to Mia. Rather than attempting to please others, or being impelled to change because she felt she 'ought to', she wanted to achieve this goal for herself, and felt entirely motivated to doing so. She understood that there would be many challenges along the way, but felt excited at the prospect of change; it made sense to her, as though things 'clicked into place' – it simply felt 'right'. Mia was completely committed to her goal and embraced the 'butterflies in her stomach' – the sense of energy – that came to the fore when she thought about it.

Similar to Mia, Duncan could no longer tolerate the feeling of discomfort and dissatisfaction; he no longer wanted to waste his life and felt a compulsion to change. His goal was to learn how to feel comfortable in his own skin. Placing this goal in the context of his life in general, Duncan felt that he would become more effective both at work and socially by becoming less dependent on others' approval. He was motivated by his desire to move beyond his sadness over the ending of his relationship with Jenny, to once more move out of his parents' home and establish his independence, and to forge new and meaningful relationships with others. He felt the rewards would be many. He would no longer need to turn to chocolate as a crutch and so be able to better control his weight, he would no longer need to buy clothes to enhance his attractiveness, he would be able to sleep more soundly through the night and so perform more efficiently at work, and would be able to really start living.

With his goal in mind, I devised a treatment programme for Duncan that was to include 10 one-to-one hypnotherapy sessions over a four-month period.

Being fully aware of the rewards, Duncan too wanted to achieve his goal. He was doing this for himself. He had a very realistic approach to the change process and recognised that he would face many demanding times ahead, times that would possibly stretch him to his limits. But, because he was completely committed to making his goal his reality, he decided to engage wholeheartedly with the change process. He chose to take full responsibility for what he was going to do from here, to be disciplined in his approach, and to learn from any mistakes made. He described feeling 'like an adult' for the first time in his life; he felt ready and willing to take action to make permanent changes. As with Mia, Duncan also felt the energy of excitement as his confidence and belief in himself started to take root through new experience. He was buzzing, and he loved the feeling – he was 'alive'.

What is your goal/what specifically do you want to achieve? Be as detailed as you can.

Thinking more broadly about your goal state:

- **How would you like to feel?**
- **What thoughts would you like to think?**
- **How would you like to behave?**

What are your motivations for your goal?

What are the likely rewards of achieving this goal?

What actions will you need to take to achieve your goal?

What personal skills will you need to draw upon to make this goal your reality?

What external sources of support will you need? Are these available to you? If not, what can you do about this?

Given your current life and your responsibilities within it, is this goal realistic and attainable? Is now the right time?

How does achieving this goal fit in with the bigger picture of your life?

When you've achieved your goal, how will your life differ from how it is now?

How committed do you feel toward making this goal your reality? If not 100%, what is stopping your from committing fully?

How will you measure your progress? (Perhaps the answer to this question could be, 'I will monitor my success at the end of each chapter.')

How long do you anticipate it will take to achieve this goal? (A reasonable time-frame for your goal achievement could be the period of time it takes you to complete this book. Decide how much time per day/week you will devote to this process and stick to your decision.)

How will you know when you have achieved your goal?

To further cement your goal and explore any obstacles that might hinder your success, cue Audio 2 – Visualising my goal.

Having listened to the recording, now summarise your goal as a mission statement (a short, simple statement that outlines your intention).

So, you know how the sense of discomfort is affecting you in the present and you have a firm goal regarding how you'd like to be and feel instead. Now it's time to investigate that old feeling of discomfort in more detail with a view to beginning the process of changing it.

Progress report:

My expectations: You now have a clearer understanding of what the discomfort is, what's currently contributing to it, and how it's affecting you and your life. You have set the specifics of your goal and believe it to be attainable, relevant and measurable. You are aware of your time-frame for achieving the goal. You are making practical adjustments regarding any life-style issues that might be impacting the current state of discomfort.

What you've learned:

How this knowledge affects your perception of the discomfort and dissatisfaction you're currently experiencing:

Chapter 5

The change process continues – parts therapy

We're now going to further explore your feelings of discomfort through parts therapy. You may remember what parts therapy is, but if not, take a quick look back to pages 43–44 to remind yourself. This may well seem like a small chapter; in terms of the number of pages, it is. But, in terms of its therapeutic value and relevance to the process of change, this is far from the case. Its major contribution rests in what results from having listened to the audio (Audio 3).

N.B. It is important to recognise that the parts of us that end up generating internal conflict are not acting in deliberately antagonistic ways toward us; they do not represent 'enemies' to be fought and defeated, or irritants to be ignored. Rather, these parts represent either useful messages that something in our lives needs our attention, or, more typically, they represent past coping strategies that came into being with the sole purpose of helping us adapt to and survive difficult circumstances. Either way, when these parts first emerged, they had very positive intentions for us. And, because they were so useful to us at the time, these parts have endured, unaltered to influence today. Parts therapy facilitates a re-education of these well-intentioned but now out-dated ways of being, harnessing their energy and re-directing it to more useful ends.

When did you first became aware of feeling uncomfortable and dissatisfied with your life? What was going on in your life at that time?

Initially, Mia felt that her sense of discomfort was easy to identify.

Due to becoming pregnant aged 20, Mia, now 30, no longer recognised herself; 'I just don't know who I am any more'. She described the feeling as that of stress. It was a heavy, knotted, dark, ominous sensation that dwelt in her lower stomach, similar, she said, to extreme hunger pains. She was continually aware of its presence (6/10) but it was particularly strongly felt when she had to make decisions (10/10).

Through parts therapy, however, she was able to understand that these feelings first emerged when she was 5 years old; her parents' marriage had begun to break down at this time and her once secure home-life had become problematic. On questioning the part that generated these uncomfortable feelings, Mia came to understand that it did, genuinely have positive intentions for her – it was trying to alert her to her need to adapt to new circumstances. So, she thanked the stressed part for its efforts, re-educated it in relation to the discomfort it was now causing her, and assigned its energies to a new role, a role that motivated her towards taking back control of her life.

Duncan had felt this sense of disquiet about himself for as long as he could remember and was permanently very aware of it at a 10/10 level; even at nursery school he remembers feeling isolated and different from the other children.

Through parts therapy, he learned that he mostly experienced this discomfort in his chest and stomach; that it felt like a cold, massive void, a deep, dark, heavy emptiness inside; it felt hopeless. He first became aware of this sensation on his first day at nursery school when his adoptive mother left him without saying goodbye. He remembers the panic, the terror. He knew no one there. He felt completely alone. So, he bided his time, 'playing' alone until he could leave. This coping strategy continued throughout his education and into adulthood, expecting nothing from others and applying himself to learning. Duncan was able to see that this part had simply been trying to help him survive a very challenging situation, providing distraction through focus, so, he was able to acknowledge its efforts, re-educate it and re-direct its energies toward helping him accept himself for who he was.

🎧 To help you explore and begin to re-educate what might be generating your sense of discomfort, cue Audio 3 – Re-educating the mind through parts therapy.

Now that you've listened to the recording, write down all that you've discovered about your sense of discomfort – amongst other things, how it feels, what it represents, what its positive intentions are, when you first became aware of it, what new role you've decided it could now take.

Progress report:

My expectations: You now have an even clearer understanding of the discomfort you were feeling and have re-educated the part of you that generated that discomfort. You have decided on a new, more helpful role for that old part to play.

What you've learned:

How this knowledge affects your perception of the discomfort and dissatisfaction:

Chapter 6

Anchoring – generating calm physical control at your fingertips

You will now have a better understanding of that old sense of discomfort, you have your goal at the forefront of your mind, and you have identified any obstacles that could hinder your success. You've also begun the process of changing that sense of discomfort. The chief aim of this next stage of the change process is to enable you to retain a sense of physical and emotional ease in any given situation.

Knowing that how we feel influences how we behave, we're now going to move on to address the detrimental physical and emotional symptoms that are generated by your sense of discomfort and dissatisfaction (the physical and emotional symptoms you identified in Chapter 4).

At this point in the development plan, doubts and fatigue can start creeping in. The goal can feel like climbing to the top of Everest with very sore knees, altitude sickness and oxygen canisters that are running low. So, another aim of this chapter is to give you a bit of a break from self-reflection.

Anchoring

You are already working on generating physical comfort by deepening and slowing your breath through the 5/7 method of breathing. Breathing in such a way switches on the para-sympathetic nervous system (the opposite system to the one that generates physical discomfort – the sympathetic nervous system). Keep practising – this is the first step to maintaining control of your body.

But there's so much more that you can do to develop and retain physical and emotional comfort. From Chapter 1, we know that the unconscious mind and the internal body systems are linked, so, we're going to use this knowledge to good effect, override old, habitual *detrimental* physical and emotional responses, and provide you with a new resourceful, calm state of being via a method called Anchoring. (To remind yourself what Anchoring is, please refer back to Chapter 2.)

This is the theoretical basis of Anchoring: We are learning all the time, even when we're not consciously aware of it. One of the simplest ways in which we learn is through association (Behaviourists refer to it as 'Classical Conditioning'), linking one thing with another: x is followed by y; the colour red suggests danger; a crime is followed by a punishment; grey hair suggests old age (darn cheek; I started going grey when I was 21). Here, x, red, crime and grey hair are the stimulus (the anchor/trigger) to y, danger, punishment and old age (the response). Neurological pathways form in the unconscious mind linking these associations. These associations, when triggered, inform situation dependent automatic physical, emotional and behavioural responses.

Let me explain further: Where your sense of discomfort

is concerned, the way in which your body responds to life's difficulties is based upon stored associations, associations that are housed in your unconscious mind. Once formed, whether they're right or wrong, beneficial or not, these neurological pathways automatically inform your current response to similar situations. Let's say you've formed an association between spiders and fear; when you encounter a spider, without having the time to think about it, you instantly start shaking, you're nauseous and your heart pumps so violently you believe it will burst through your rib cage; you feel terrified; more than likely you run away from the spider.

It was the Behaviourist, Pavlov (and, of course, his hungry, salivating dog) who first brought this way of learning to our attention. Under laboratory conditions, the hungry dog was brought food. It was noted that the dog's automatic physiological response to the provision of the food was to salivate. Then, over several sessions, just before the delivery of the food, a bell rang. Gradually the dog learned that the bell signalled the imminent arrival of the food, the eventual result being that when the bell rang on its own, the dog salivated – it had learned that the bell and the provision of food were associated. No dog would salivate on simply hearing a bell ringing unless it had previously learned that the bell and the food were linked.

We can learn these associations through gradual exposure to them (as in the case of Pavlov's dog) or through powerful one-off experiences of them. For example, as a child you might have had your head dunked under water by a well-intentioned, playful adult whilst at your local swimming baths. You were terrified out of your wits.

Because of the intensity of the experience, you learned instantly that water is frightening.

Throughout our lives we learn to associate emotional, physical and behavioural responses to specific experiences and situations. Some of these responses are enjoyable and beneficial, some quite the opposite.

For example, a particular song was played just once on that wonderful evening out with a fabulous friend. You instantly associated that piece of music with the joy you experienced on the evening out. So, on hearing the song again (the stimulus/anchor), in any context, you will, most likely, experience feelings of happiness (the learned emotional response). The hearing of another song, however, one that you used to play over and over whilst revising for exams many years ago, will probably result in feelings of disquiet or anxiety.

You were hungry one lunchtime and left work to grab a pizza. A couple of hours later you were violently vomiting in the staff toilets in terrible pain, having already re-decorated your desk. Because of the powerful nature of the experience, you instantly learned to associate pizza with pain and sickness. A few months later, a friend invites you round for a meal – they've cooked pizza (the stimulus). You are polite and try your best not to offend your friend, but, even before the first bite, you feel sick and your stomach hurts (learned physical response).

One of the most prevalent phobias within Western societies is glossophobia – the fear of public speaking. There can be many causes for such a fear developing, yet, one of the most common rests on past difficult experiences of presenting, and the association of speaking in front of others with anxiety and fear. When I was at school, we were often made to read aloud in class by a particularly cruel, unpredictably explosive old-school English teacher who we all aptly nicknamed Miss Timebomb. She seemed to revel in pouncing on the most shy and retiring in the class to read passages of worthy text aloud to the rest of us. Victims would stutter and stumble their way through the words, their fight/flight/freeze response well and truly triggered. The rest of the class would stifle titters of derision at the sheer lack of literary competence of the reader. Souls such as these will have learned over time that public speaking is a terrifying ordeal to be avoided at all costs. Stimulus: Speaking in public. Learned emotional response: Fear and anxiety. Consequential behavioural response: Avoid.

But, just as unhealthy associations that negatively affect our emotions and bodies can be created, they can be overridden by generating new neurological pathways in the brain. Hooray!

This is how: By associating a resourceful emotional and physical state (calm comfort, for example) to a particular anchor, a new neurological pathway can be established that will overrule old, unhelpful patterns of response. In this way, we can choose a more appropriate, comfortable way of dealing with things. Let's take the fear of spiders example to demonstrate this: By linking the spider with calm interest, the old neurological pathway that associated spiders with fear can be overridden.

As already mentioned in Chapter 2, my preferred anchor, the anchor I teach to my clients, focuses on the sense of touch. It is one that involves the person's dominant hand, the hand they typically trust and depend on. Should I encounter someone who is ambidextrous, either hand would suffice. Because the touch receptors are particularly sensitive in the fingertips, I ask each person to gently bring the thumb and index finger together to form a circle. It's a subtle gesture that can be done discretely. Some anchors involve the making of a fist. However, I for one know that when I make a fist, or see someone else making a fist, I immediately associate it with aggression. Plus, for anyone with long nails, making a fist can hurt.

Once your anchor has been installed (via Audio 4 – Self-control at my fingertips), it's vital to understand is that the power contained within it will not run out. In fact, the more you use it, the stronger the neural pathway that links the anchor to your desired response state becomes, and the more effective it is.

We now know what the anchor's going to be – the gentle pressing together of the thumb and index finger of the dominant hand – but, what resourceful state do we want to associate it with? What will be most useful to you in your day-to-day life? Given your current issue of feeling uncomfortable, I'm assuming that a greater sense of inner comfort wouldn't go amiss, a sense of ease within self. So, calm comfort at your fingertips it is.

🎧 Instilling your anchor, cue Audio 4 – Self-control at my fingertips.

N.B. In the future, please do not wait until you're feeling very uncomfortable before using your anchor; the most effective time to employ it is at the *very first sign* of any physical or emotional discomfort.

Progress report:

My expectations: You now have a growing sense of confidence in your ability to generate emotional and physical control at will, to then choose to react calmly and comfortably to any given situation. You will practise your skill often and, when required, employ your anchor at the very first sign of any sense of discomfort – through practice, you'll make it work for you.

What you've learned:

How this knowledge affects your perception of the discomfort and dissatisfaction:

Chapter 7

How did you get to this point? Identifying and addressing potential historical causes

Shall I compare thee to an onion? Rude of me, I know, for thou art more lovely, and far less pungent, I'm sure.

But, forgive me; such an analogy is useful because it illustrates the fact that each individual's issue is, more often than not, multi-layered and that these layers typically conceal an important central something, a something that probably stems from a seed that was sown much earlier in your life. It is possible that there are no historical causes for this sense of discomfort you're currently feeling, but, from my experience, a thorough exploration of a person's past, although demanding, is incredibly eye opening and beneficial in the long-run.

A client may present with a particular issue, but, if we simply took that issue at face value and dealt only with it, we might be missing the underlying cause and the problem would almost certainly return – a bit like painting over old wallpaper ... When my husband was a young child, his bedroom walls were adorned with Noddy wallpaper; every six inches or so, a bright, bold picture of a lad in a blue hat and red jacket looked out at him cheerily. As he grew older, Noddy became passé (rather embarrassing really), and his parents agreed to re-decorate his room. They bought the paint and covered over each and every little Noddy figure. However, as the months passed, hundreds of little blue hats began to re-emerge.

Remember Mia; she was convinced that her current sense of discomfort was related to her pregnancy. It was only on further reflection that she uncovered the true cause when, at the age of 5, her life as she knew it, was turned upside down by her parents' relationship difficulties.

Ideally, we want to get to the core, the historical heart of the matter, the root cause of your sense of discomfort.

In order to do this, let's go back to the beginning of your story, back to your specific experiences of being socialised and nurtured. (Remembering that the conscious mind doesn't begin developing until about the age of two, our very early experiences are of immense relevance here, for our unconscious mind simply absorbed in a sponge-like fashion everything we experienced from birth to that point, forming the foundations of our beliefs about ourselves, others and our place in the world.)

'Socialisation' is the process by which we acquire a personal identity, learning the language, norms, customs, values and ideologies of the culture into which we're born, developing the social skills necessary to function within that society. 'Nurture' refers to the care we receive while we're growing.

Socialisation

Think about and describe the chief elements of the society into which you were born. What were the major values and beliefs?

For example, and, in brief: I was born into 1964 Cold War (possibly nuclear war) Britain, a culture in which the class system was strong, and sexism, racism, religious intolerance and homophobia were rife. Abortion and homosexuality were illegal and the death sentence was meted out for those who committed murder. Men and women had very clear gender roles. Little was known about child psychology. It was culturally accepted that stable families were vital to a stable society, that marriage was necessary, and that divorce was socially undesirable. The Vietnam War was raging and Mods and Rockers were fighting. On a brighter note, conscription had ended, 'flower power' blossomed, the teenager was born, and there was a revolution in music that accompanied massive technological advancement.

In relation to being either female or male, when you were growing up, what gender expectations were placed on you and how did these influence your development?

What role did your class/social status and education play in your upbringing and on your development?

What role did your race or ethnicity play in your upbringing and on your development?

What role did religion play in your upbringing and on your development?

What other aspects of the society into which you were born had an impact on you? How did they influence your development?

Nurture

Following John Bowlby's research in Child Development, the developmental psychologist Mary Ainsworth added greatly to our understanding of the factors that influence early childhood development. Her research led to the formation of Attachment Theory, a theory that is as relevant today in explaining individual differences as it was when she conducted her Strange Situation experiments back in the 1970s.

The premises of Attachment Theory are as follows: Regarding our experiences of being nurtured, we are born completely dependent upon the care of others – our primary caregivers (from here-on known as PCs). This first relationship plays a central role in our psychological development. We look to our PC (typically, although not exclusively, the mother) not only to take care of our physiological needs, but also to provide for our psychological needs, looking to them for protection from harm, desiring to remain close to them for maximum protection, and turning to them for comfort when we're upset. This relationship is so fundamental to our survival that, to maintain the relationship, we learn to adapt our behaviour to compliment theirs, quickly learning to mould our behaviour to match the PC's expectations and ways of doing things. Based on how available the PC is to us, how attuned they are to satisfying our physiological and emotional needs, we form belief systems concerning who we are, who we are in relation to others and who the other is. We rapidly develop expectations of the relationship.

Attachment Theory categorises four types of attachment; secure, insecure-ambivalent, insecure-avoidant, and disorganised.

Should our PC be dependably warm, loving and attuned to meeting our infant needs on a consistent basis, we are likely to develop a sense of physical and emotional safety. We grow up with a balanced, healthy regard for ourselves and for others. Such inner security acts as a safe base from which we are able to explore the world around us and develop as a person. Emotions such as anger do not adversely impact the relationship, but are accepted as being normal. In psychological terms this pattern of early experience is referred to as secure attachment.

If our PC is unpredictable and inconsistent in their care for and attentiveness to us, overly aware of their own problems and not fully attuned to our infant needs, we typically grow up with a sense of insecurity about who we are, what we're capable of and whether our needs will be prioritised, met or not. We often suffer from separation anxiety and develop behavioural coping strategies such as kicking up an almighty fuss that, in effect, force attention from the PC. As we grow, we learn that high-octane emotional displays elicit attention from others. We learn to depend on others managing our problems for us.

This pattern of early experience is referred to as insecure-ambivalent attachment.

Should our PC be hostile, rejecting, distant and uncomfortable with shows of our neediness, we quickly learn that the only way we're going to remain close to our PC, and so maximise our comfort and safety, is to shut our feelings off. As we develop further, we learn to become emotionally and physically overly self-reliant, fearful that, should we display our needs and true feelings to others, we'll be rejected. This form of attachment is called insecure-avoidant.

If our PC has unresolved painful attachment issues of their own, they can be over-whelmed by our infant needs because those needs trigger their own historical trauma. The PC is viewed by the dependent infant as a source of potential safety but also a source of definite danger. Such an approach renders the developing child with a 'fear without solution' situation, a sense of having no control for they recognise early on that there is nothing they can do to elicit attention from their PC. The child learns to shut down their emotions and needs, and lacks the opportunities to learn how to be close to others and how to cope with stressful situations. As they grow, they typically become detached from their emotions and needs and settle into a sense of hopelessness and powerlessness, understanding that others let them down and are not to be relied upon. This is referred to as disorganised attachment. Conversely, people who've experienced this form of attachment can also adopt bullying tendencies toward certain others, others they recognise as being weaker than themselves.

Let's look again at Mia. She was born in 1980 to middle-class, Conservative-voting parents. She was one of three children, having an older brother and sister. She received a good education and, although her mother wasn't particularly religious, she was regularly taken by her to a Protestant church. She absorbed many of the lessons taught by the church about morality. At University, she became interested in feminism and joined a women's group that helped her form expectations of a full and satisfying career that would provide her with financial independence and a sense of autonomy.

Despite the normal sibling rivalries, her very early years were stable and she remembers feeling loved and valued as a youngster. She experienced secure attachment with her mother. However, aged about five, her parents' marriage began to break down and arguments and tension crept into the relationship, negatively affecting the whole family. Her parents began to focus on themselves. This continued for five years until, when Mia was 10, her brother 12 and her sister 15, her parents divorced. During these difficult years, the pre-existing channels of communication between family members broke down and the family stopped talking to each other. Mia had no outlet for her worry, and the conflict that existed became a taboo subject thus remaining unresolved. Like many children whose parents get divorced, Mia believed that she was to blame. At the time of the divorce, Mia, her siblings and her mother moved out of the family home and lived in cold, inhospitable rented accommodation, Mia and her older brother spending weekends with their father back in the old family home. Mia remembered the sense of insecurity. Her mother was in much emotional pain and now lacked the resources to focus on Mia's growing needs.

A year or so later, Mia's father met and married a woman called Marlene. She had no children of her own and didn't seem to want to share her new husband with his original family. Mia described Marlene as a sly, manipulative woman who was discretely hostile towards her. When issues arose, to avoid conflict with his new wife, Mia's father openly sided with Marlene. And so the distance between Mia and her father grew. Mia remembers a sense of loss where her father was concerned, a sense of betrayal, a fear of not being able to see him, a sense of powerlessness at her inability to affect things. Although Mia had been brought up to discuss difficult emotions, after the age of 5, she quickly understood that bringing anger, conflict and fear to the mixing pot generated more stress and tension than her parents could bear, so she learned instead to bottle things up and avoid conflict.

Being influenced by coping strategies adopted by her older brother and sister, Mia realised that she was now responsible for her own success and happiness and became very driven academically, wanting to become an English teacher. She applied herself well at school and, after her A levels, began an English degree. During this time, she met and fell in love with Geoff, a Business Studies student. In her final year she accidentally fell pregnant and dropped out of University, while Geoff continued with his studies and secured himself a first class honours degree. Her life as she had foreseen it fell apart. She blamed herself wholeheartedly for this, the guilt eating her up inside, rendering her impotent to manifest change.

Duncan's story is a different one. He was born in 1967. He knows nothing of the background of his birth mother. His adoptive parents were middle-class, Labour-voting people who both shared a strong social, but not religious, conscience. Despite many years trying, his adoptive mother had been unable to have children of her own and had begun to feel inadequate because of this. Her childhood had been a cold one, but she felt desperate to have a child of her own. Once Duncan had been adopted, his adoptive mother soon became overwhelmed by his needs, which triggered strong memories of unresolved maltreatment and neglect from her own upbringing. She was able to meet his physical and academic needs, but not his emotional ones.

His adoptive parents were very open about the fact that Duncan was not their own flesh and blood; they thought this was the correct thing to do. His adoptive mother seemed distant, even hostile at times, and overly challenged by his displays of neediness. Duncan internalised this information and described how he always felt a sense of not really belonging to this family, a sense of rejection, a need to be quiet and well behaved, and a deep feeling of loss at being abandoned by his birth mother. The sense of being different to others and isolated from others had already begun to take shape. Duncan experienced insecure-avoidant attachment with his 'mother'.

As he grew, to protect his 'mother' from the burden of the truth of his loneliness and to protect himself from the dreadful feelings that such loneliness caused, Duncan learned to put on a mask, to pretend that he was okay. He felt he was acting his way through life; that he was a fraud. Duncan was a very academically able child and this ability, again, differentiated and separated him from others at school. He did make a couple of friends, but was bullied by his peers throughout his school days. Duncan's sense of being different to others was thus regularly reinforced.

Duncan blamed his birth mother for giving him away and felt fury at the injustice of her desertion. He blamed his adoptive mother for not loving him and felt that he had become a shadow of what he might have otherwise been. He blamed his teachers for failing in their duty to nurture his academic abilities (being one in a class of 30+, they simply didn't have the time to focus on his needs), and he blamed the children who bullied him for tormenting him for all those years. He saw himself as hopeless and powerless to generate change and felt that life just happened to and around him.

The following questions ask you to consider your experiences of being nurtured. In allowing yourself to respond openly and honestly about these experiences, you might well begin to feel uncomfortable and guilty, feeling perhaps that you're blaming your parents for things that happened or being disloyal in some way. However, worry not; by responding to the following questions, you are not laying any blame at anyone's feet (unless it feels appropriate to do so), you are not criticising or being disloyal, you are simply detailing your perceptions of those early experiences and acknowledging the effect they had on you.

Let's now consider your nurture experiences:

Who was your primary caregiver?

Did you feel safe with them?

Did they enable you to be physically close to them?

Did you feel able to turn to them when you were upset?

Were they highly aware of your infant needs? Or, were their needs more important than yours?

How would you describe their approach to you (warm, unpredictable, loving, hostile, dependable, remote, secure, fearful, enjoyable, inconsistent, encouraging, preoccupied with self, frightening, accepting, rejecting)?

How would you describe your attachment with your PC (secure, insecure-avoidant, insecure-ambivalent, disorganised)?

What did you learn about your individual value from these experiences with your PC?

How did these early experiences with your PC influence your emotions and your behaviour?

On a day-to-day basis, would you describe your typical reactions to events, people and situations as more emotional than logical or the other way around? What are the consequences of this?

What, if any, impact do these early experiences with your PC have on your current life, your behaviour and your relationships with others?

How did your relationship with your PC change over time? If they are still living, what is your relationship with them now?

If the relationship is now a beneficial one and was not so before, how did this change come about?

This very early relationship with our PC will have had a marked effect on our psychological development. But, of course, as time passes, we begin to form other relationships, relationships with siblings, other relatives, friends and various figures of authority.

In relation to our birth order, first-borns typically adapt themselves most to their parents' expectations. They tend to get undivided attention from their parents and achieve well academically, securing satisfying careers for themselves – many leaders are first-borns. They become adults who are conscientious, ambitious, responsible, and organised. First-borns can feel intensely the loss of attention that results from the arrival of their siblings.

Later children tend to identify less with their parents

and, because they are forced to submit to their older siblings, often develop a strong sense of empathy toward the underdog. They tend to resist authority and conformity and can be seen by their parents as rebels. They are often less confident but more sociable people than older siblings.

A middle child can often feel the most overlooked by their parents, squeezed between the needs of the first-born high achiever, and the 'baby' of the family, resulting in adults who suffer from low self-esteem, jealousy, feelings of inadequacy and a tendency to be introverted.

If you have brothers and sisters, what was your birth order? From your own experience, what was the impact of growing up in this order? How did your birth order influence your development to adulthood?

Were there different expectations placed on your siblings to you?

Did your parents treat your siblings differently to you? Were some siblings more favoured than others? If so, what impact did this have on you?

What did you learn about yourself as you grew up in relation to your siblings?

If you were an only child, how did you feel about this and how did it affect you as you were growing up? What role/s were you expected to play within the family?

What did you learn from the family you grew up in about your attractiveness, your intelligence, your gender role, your sexual orientation, your strengths, your weaknesses, managing conflict, jealousy, pain and anger?

What kind of things did you get reprimanded for? How were you reprimanded? What effect did this have on your development?

What kind of things were you praised for? How were you praised? What effect did this have on your development?

How would you describe your parents' relationship? As you grew, how did their relationship change?

What did you learn about relationships from witnessing your parents' relationship?

Think about friendships you made (and lost) over time; reflect on significant others (relatives and romantic/sexual partners, figures of authority) in your life who were influential in your further development. What did you learn about yourself and others through these relationships? In what ways did these relationships confirm or challenge your views?

As we grow, our experiences broaden. We go to school, we change schools, we make friends, we lose friends, we might move house, loved ones may become ill or die, our own health might become problematic, we discover our own sexual identity, adolescence hits and our bodies change, we experiment, we take exams, we make mistakes, we fail and we succeed, we learn to drive, we leave home, we get a job or study further, we commit to lasting relationships, we have children, we get divorced and so on.

Spend some time reflecting back on your life and draw a time line (a linear representation of important events in the order in which they occurred) of relationships, events and experiences that you had from birth to date. Then, think about how these relationships, experiences and events impacted your emotions, your behaviour, your view of yourself, your view of other people, and your view of your place in the world.

Did anything specific happen during your childhood that you feel had an impact on this current sense of discomfort emerging?

Is there anyone or anything from your past that you blame/hold responsible for your present feeling of discomfort?

Reflect back over your responses to the questions above and to the insights gained from Audio 3 – the parts therapy audio, and identify, if there is one, the root cause of your sense of discomfort. This will form the focus of the next hypnosis session.

If you cannot identify a root cause for your current sense of discomfort, with the upcoming audio in mind, select a notable uncomfortable past experience that you believe is negatively impacting the present.

Please note: If these questions have uncovered once repressed memories of abuse, violence or trauma, or have revealed very painful memories, do not listen to Audio 5. Rather, see a professional clinical hypnotherapist for one-to-one sessions, to guide you carefully through your past issues.

🎧 Armed with the memory of the root cause of your discomfort or a notable uncomfortable past experience, cue regression Audio 5 – Laying the past to rest.

N.B. It is possible, through Regression hypnosis, for once repressed memories to come to the fore. Although potentially uncomfortable, if this happens, see it as a highly positive step forward, a sign that your unconscious mind is now ready to begin dealing with difficult past issues. It is also possible for factually incorrect memories to arise, memories of things that feel accurate but that didn't actually happen – this is called False Memory Syndrome. Should Audio 5 have uncovered memories that are overly troubling, whether those memories are real or not, as soon as you're able to do so, make an appointment to see a qualified clinical hypnotherapist to help you work it through.

If you live in Great Britain, to find a qualified, accredited clinical hypnotherapist operating in your area contact:

The General Hypnotherapy Register (GHR): www. general-hypnotherapy-register.com

Together, the General Hypnotherapy Standards Council (GHSC) and the GHR are the UK's largest and most prominent organisation within the field of hypnotherapy and present an exemplary model for the simultaneous protection of the public and the provision of practitioner credibility and services.

Should you live outside the UK, using the words 'hypnotherapy register' in your search engine, find the national register of hypnotherapists relevant to your location.

Progress report:

My expectations: You now have a better understanding of the historical causes of that old sense of discomfort and have modified their impact on present life through Regression hypnosis.

What you've learned:

How this knowledge affects your perception of the discomfort and dissatisfaction:

Chapter 8

Transforming detrimental core beliefs

To be perfectly honest, this chapter is challenging; challenging in that it requires you to become consciously aware of things that reside deep within the unconscious mind. Sorry! However, I encourage you to *take your time* and work your way through it; it is a pivotal part of the change process. By way of reassurance, I take every client who comes to see me through this procedure and each person has emerged far more knowledgeable for their efforts. Just take it step by step knowing that you simply need to put one foot in front of the other to make progress.

Amalgamating and adapting Rational Emotive Behavioural Therapy (REBT) developed by Albert Ellis (1950s), and Cognitive Behavioural Therapy (CBT) created by Aaron T. Beck (1960s), the focus of this chapter centres on the understanding that the core beliefs we hold influence how we interpret things that happen in our lives and how we then respond to them; 'we do not approach situations neutrally as we bring with us our core beliefs' (Dryden, 2000). For example, someone holding very destructive beliefs about themselves and the world in which they live is more than likely going to see themselves as helpless, triggering possible negative emotions such as depression, and behavioural responses such as withdrawal from life.

The goal of this chapter is to identify and transform specific core beliefs that are having a detrimental effect on your sense of comfort in and satisfaction with life.

So then, what are core beliefs? Core beliefs are 'truths' that we hold at an unconscious level of mind about who we are, what we're capable of, who we are in relation to others, and what our place is in the world around us. 'I'm attractive', 'Others are better than me', I'm clever' and 'It's wrong to steal' are all examples of core beliefs. They act as internal working models or templates of behavioural response that require no conscious input. They help us structure the world in which we live and automatically navigate our way through life.

Our core beliefs develop over time as a result of the period into which we're born, the culture we grow up in and our own personal set of relationships and experiences. Because our core beliefs are stored in the unconscious part of the mind we are blissfully unaware of their existence. When we do become aware of them, we generally identify them as indisputable 'facts' about 'how things are'. As a result, whether they are accurate or not, we do not question our core beliefs and simply allow them to continue to influence our lives. But, we were not born holding these core beliefs, we learned them, so, if they're negatively affecting our lives, it stands to reason that we can change them, and that we will benefit from doing so.

Based on our core beliefs we make automatic inferences and assumptions about specific current events and our ability to handle them. In a mere nanosecond, the inferences we make inform our thought processes concerning the events. These thoughts are neither reasoned nor reflective in that they bypass the conscious mind, yet they spontaneously determine how we feel about those current situations and how we're going to behave toward them, to our benefit or to our detriment.

It is because we all hold individually specific core beliefs that two people can have very different responses to the same situation. My husband and I have many things in common, but, when faced with an opportunity to go clothes shopping, we react very differently. Experience has taught me that clothes shopping is, on the whole, a joy; I believe it will give me pleasure, therefore, I want to do it and, when the opportunity arises, I go clothes shopping. Charlie, on the other hand, has formed the belief that clothes shopping is a pain in the proverbial; the thought of it makes him stressed – he does not want to do it, and avoids going by adding his requirements to my list.

Healthy core beliefs (beliefs such as 'I can' and 'I'm resourceful') will typically have a very beneficial effect on our lives, generating thoughts that help us achieve our goals with the maximum of ease and comfort. But, unhealthy, rigidly-held core beliefs (such as 'I can't' or 'I'm stupid') typically generate dysfunctional and self-defeating thoughts that are:

- Negative in nature
- Irrational (fuelled by 'what ifs')
- Assumption-based (you make assumptions and take these assumptions as fact, even though they're only guesses about what might be)
- Demanding (should, ought)

- Inflexible (must, have to)
- Intolerant (can't stand this)
- Polarised (black and white, right and wrong)
- Catastrophising (exaggerating)
- Fixated (disproportionate focus)
- Deprecating (you or I are less of a person if...).

Not surprisingly, this style of thinking tends to limit our lives and our sense of safety and comfort in the world.

Let's take a look at how a detrimental core belief can inform our thoughts, feelings and behaviour in a given situation – delivering a presentation. There's a clear 'top-down' process for how this works:

Over time, based on your interactions and experiences, you have formed the core belief 'I'm a useless presenter':

1. An event occurs in the here and now – at work you are asked to deliver a presentation (the Activating Event)

2. Triggered by the above core belief, dysfunctional thoughts about your ability to deliver the presentation automatically flow, thoughts that are typically:

   - *Irrational/untruthful*: 'I can't do it'
   - *Demanding*: 'I've got to do it'
   - *Inflexible*: 'I have to deliver the perfect presentation'
   - *Intolerant*: 'I can't stand this'
   - *Assumption*: 'I won't be able to do it'
   - *Fixated*: 'Nothing is as important as this'
   - *Exaggerated/catastrophising*: 'It'll be a complete failure and I'll look ridiculous'

- *Deprecating*: 'I'm a failure'

These thoughts are automatically, instantly reinforced by memories of past 'failures' where presenting is concerned.

3. The thoughts affect your emotional and physical state concerning the presentation – discomfort and dread – triggering the flight/fight/freeze (stress) response, rendering your ability to present effectively even less likely.

4. Your emotional and physical state in turn informs your behavioural response to the event – possibly that of avoidance or, if the presentation goes ahead, under-performance.

5. What's more, in an attempt to cope with the emotional discomfort you may adopt harmful and self-defeating behaviours, such as smoking, drinking too much, comfort eating, self-sabotaging and so on. A downward spiral is created in which you find your detrimental core belief further reinforced.

When we find ourselves feeling negatively toward a specific situation, it's key to understand that it is not the situation itself that has disturbed us, rather it's the beliefs we hold about our capacity to deal with the situation effectively that causes us the distress.

For those of you who understand things more clearly from a visual perspective, the process looks like this:

Transforming detrimental core beliefs

1. ACTIVATING EVENT you are asked to deliver a presentation

This instantly triggers the rigidly held **DETRIMENTAL CORE BELIEF**

> I'm a useless presenter

2. DYSFUNCTIONAL THOUGHTS (informed by the core belief)

> I ought to be able to do it but I can't; I must do it even though it'll be a complete failure; I'm useless at my job; it feels like the end of the world

RE-INFORCED BY:

> memories of past difficult presenting experiences

PHYSICAL RESPONSES:

> sweating, breathlessness, shaking, nausea, pounding heart, brain freeze

3. EMOTIONAL STATE (fed by the thoughts)

> anxiety

4. BEHAVIOURS/CONSEQUENCES (informed by the emotional state)

> avoidance or ineffective delivery of presentation; perpetuation of the core belief; once away from the situation, you light up a cigarette/drink alcohol/ eat chocolate, etc.

Let's consider Mia and Duncan's core beliefs.

Because Mia blames herself for her parents' divorce, she has formed the core belief 'It's all my fault'. Such a belief has diminished her confidence in herself as a capable, decisive adult.

1.   Current Activating Event: Geoff asks Mia to investigate the local schools to then make a decision regarding the best option for their two children to attend. He hasn't got the time to do it himself.

This current situation triggers...

2.   Unhealthy/unhelpful automatic thoughts:

   •   'I'm not capable of making this decision.' (untruthful and illogical)
   •   I must make the right decision for my children.' (demanding)
   •   'If I did get it wrong, I'd be ruining the children's lives and Geoff would think I'm utterly useless. They'd never forgive me.'(catastrophising)
   •   'I can't stand this responsibility.' (intolerant/inflexible)
   •   'Geoff and my children would see me as the stupid person that I am if I made the wrong decision.' (self-deprecating)
   •   'I'll make the wrong decision. I've been wrong before as Geoff has so very kindly pointed out.' (past re-inforcement)
   •   'Oh no; it's happening to me again. Geoff is forcing me to do this.' (being 'at effect' in life)

These thoughts trigger the...

3.   Emotional state: Stress and guilt (unhealthy and unhelpful); created not by the event itself, but by the irrational, demanding and catastrophising thoughts triggered by the core belief 'It's all my fault'.

Resulting physical sensations: Sweating, heart pounding, nausea and indigestion, breathlessness, muscle tension, headaches, shaking, and so on.

4.   Resulting behaviour: By focusing on her physical discomfort and assuming that she is unwell, Mia avoids having to make the decision by taking to her bed and asking her mother to do it for her instead. In her own eyes Mia has failed to handle this situation effectively and she feels at fault. Thus, Mia's belief that 'it's all her fault' is compounded.

... by responding in this way, as Mia has done many times before, the unhelpful core belief is perpetuated and further reinforced.

Duncan's coping strategy of putting on a mask to hide his true feelings led him to form the core belief 'I'm a fraud'. This belief created a sense of fear at the possibility of being found out.

1.   Current Activating Event: Duncan is invited to a works do. He is lonely and craves others' company so, in many ways, wants to go. But, his core belief, 'I'm a fraud' is strong.

This current situation triggers...

2.   Unhealthy/unhelpful automatic thoughts:

   •   'I'm fake and others will easily find it out.' (untruthful and illogical)
   •   'I must not be found out.' (demanding)
   •   'If I was, it really would be the end of the world to me.' (catastrophising)
   •   'I just couldn't bear the shame.' (intolerant/inflexible)
   •   'If I went, others would see me for the fake that I am.' (self-deprecating)
   •   'I've faked things before.' (past re-inforcement)
   •   'There's just nothing I can do about it now.' (being 'at effect' in life)

These thoughts trigger the…

3. Emotional state: Fear (unhealthy and unhelpful); created not by the event itself, but by the irrational, demanding and 'catastrophising' thoughts triggered by the core belief 'I'm a fraud'.

    Resulting physical sensations: Sweating, heart pounding, muscle tension, nausea, shaking, and so on.

4. Resulting behaviour: Duncan turns down the invitation making up an excuse for not attending (he is fully aware of telling a lie here) and spends a few sleepless nights worrying about it. Thus, Duncan's belief 'I'm a fraud' is compounded, as is his sense of loneliness, and his desire to comfort himself with chocolate increases.

… by responding in this way, as Duncan has done many times before, the unhelpful core belief is perpetuated and further reinforced so constraining future opportunities.

And now for the really challenging part: *identifying your own core beliefs.*

As already mentioned, we tend not to be consciously aware of our core beliefs, so identifying them can be a difficult task. But it's also an important one; becoming aware of your core beliefs is the first step to changing them.

Remind yourself of what a core belief is and then, to help you begin to isolate your own 'truths', follow the steps below:

1. First think about your personality and the

perceptions you have about yourself in general and about your strengths and weaknesses.

2. Then reflect on specific situations and how you typically respond to them. What core beliefs have you formed about who you are and what you can and can't do?

3. Reflect on the roles you play in life (husband/ wife/partner, father/mother, son/daughter, employee/employer, carer, friend, etc., etc.) and begin to identify the beliefs that drive your thoughts, emotions, bodily responses and behaviours within each of these roles. For example, within your work role, what is your work ethic? What rules have you formulated about your work-life balance? As a husband/ wife, what core beliefs do you hold about trust, loyalty, respect, sex, and so on. What are your 'rules'/beliefs regarding friendship? If you are a carer, what aspects of this role are determined by your ethical codes?

4. Now think at a broader level about the principles, morals and ethics that you hold about yourself, other people and about the world around you. For example, what is good or bad, right or wrong, desirable or undesirable

about duty, equality, justice, war, poverty, religion, education, politics, sexuality and so on.

Now that you have more of an understanding of your own personal set of core beliefs, it's time to begin identifying the ones that are currently having a detrimental effect on your life.

If this seems difficult, try approaching the task from the 'bottom up'; pinpoint past situations that have triggered discomfort and then reflect on the thought processes that accompanied these feelings. Once you've identified the irrational, demanding, inflexible, intolerant, fixated, assumption-based, catastrophising, deprecating thoughts, start grouping similar ones together. Once you have certain categories of thoughts then begin to recognise the core belief(s) that lie behind them.

To help you begin to identify your set of detrimental core beliefs, listed opposite are 30 very common unhealthy core beliefs. Identify the ones that apply to you, and add your own to the list.

30 PRIMARY UNHEALTHY/ UNHELPFUL CORE BELIEFS

I'm not good enough

I'm a failure

I'm guilty

I'm unlovable

Life is hard

Others before me

I don't perform well under stress

I'm not wanted

Life is unfair

I'm not included

There's never enough

The worst always happens

I'm a fraud

I have very little control over my life

I don't function well on my own

I'm a victim

I don't deserve

I have no confidence

I'm unattractive

I'm powerless

I'm stupid

I'm a disappointment

It's better not to start

I can't

I am an alien

It'll never pass

It's all my fault

The world is a dangerous place

I can't trust people

I don't deserve attention or respect

Examining and transforming detrimental core beliefs

For each negative core belief you currently hold, think through the following...

1. In what situations do I typically become aware of this core belief? Are there particular times when I experience it more than others? How intensely do I feel it?

2. When did I first become aware of the existence of this core belief? What was going on in my life at that time?

3. Identify the accompanying negative, irrational/untruthful, inflexible, catastrophising, assumption-based, polarised, demanding, judgemental and self-deprecating thoughts that are typically triggered by this core belief.

4. What impact does it have on my emotions, my body and my behaviour? How does this impact my life?

5. Remembering those secondary gains, is this core belief helpful to me in any way?

6. **What coping behaviours have I developed to help me tolerate these thoughts and feelings?**

7. **Now for the reality test; what proof do I have that this core belief is true; where's the evidence? Is there any rational/logical basis to it?**

8. **Given that we're often more generous in our assessment of other people than we are of ourselves, could I reach the same conclusion about another person in a similar position? What's another way of looking at it?**

9. **Now, identify examples that disprove the core belief.**

10. **With these examples in mind, identify a more truthful and rational alternative to this unhealthy core belief.**

Important here is to acknowledge that the transformation of the core belief will have more beneficial influence if it genuinely rings true to you. The conversion process is not about an immediate shift in perception from one extreme to another (let's say, moving from 'I'm a useless presenter' to 'I'm a brilliant presenter'), it's about a slow progression of allowing yourself to begin to view things more honestly, 'I can pass on information' or 'I can get better at it' or 'I'm resourceful' might be an appropriate start for you to build on as the days and weeks go by.

1. What are the thought processes that are likely to stem from this transformed core belief, thoughts that are more flexible, optimistic, accepting, approving, open-minded and preferential?

2. What are the possible emotions and behaviours/actions that are likely to stem from these new thought processes?

This is how the more beneficial approach looks:

To re-cap: Based on our experiences we form core beliefs about who we are, what we're capable of, about others and about the world in which we live. Beneficial core beliefs will enhance our lives; negative ones will constrain our lives. But, these negative core beliefs are not set in stone; they can be changed and you have begun this process of changing them.

Based on the detrimental core beliefs you've transformed, place them in order of importance and select the top 4.

With the 4 core beliefs in mind, now all you need do is lie back and listen to Audio 6 – Cementing transformed core beliefs.

Transforming detrimental core beliefs

1. ACTIVATING EVENT: you are asked to deliver a presentation

This instantly triggers the **RATIONAL CORE BELIEF**

> I'm resourceful

2. HELPFUL, TRUTHFUL THOUGHTS: (informed by the core belief)

> I'd prefer not to have to present, but, it's an important part of my job and I know I have the ability to do it; I've successfully handled difficult situations before; it's the information that's important, not my performance; each time I present, I'll learn more and get better at it

RE-INFORCED BY:

> memories of past challenging experiences and lessons learned from them

PHYSICAL RESPONSES:

> perhaps a little physical tension and discomfort at first

3. EMOTIONAL STATE (fed by the thoughts)

> Initial mild concern

4. BEHAVIOURS/CONSEQUENCES (informed by the emotional state)

> delivery of presentation; information successfully passed on to others; additional lessons learned to build further confidence

Progress report:

My expectation: You have identified and transformed old, detrimental beliefs that were negatively impacting your life and your sense of comfort in it, and now have a more truthful, useful set of core beliefs.

What you've learned:

How this knowledge affects your perception of that old discomfort and dissatisfaction:

Chapter 9

Exploring forgiveness

I cannot overstate the therapeutic value of forgiveness. My approach to this aspect of the change process has been informed predominantly by contributions made to the forgiveness debate by Eva Kor, Desmond Tutu, Marina Cantacuzino and Megan Feldman Bettencourt. Their research and personal experiences have added greatly to the pool of knowledge of what forgiveness is, how to achieve it, and what it means to us as individuals and to humanity more generally.

You might well feel that forgiveness is irrelevant to your life; that there's nothing you want to forgive or seek forgiveness for. Yet, when interacting with others, either inadvertently or deliberately, we are harmed or we do harm to others – it's a simple, albeit unfortunate, fact of life, and such harm can lead to feelings of great discomfort.

Forgiveness is a choice; it doesn't feel right for everyone. As a therapist, I neither require you to forgive, nor do I view it as your ethical duty to do so. But, when making a decision about whether to forgive or not, it's wise to make an informed choice …

Romanian born Eva Kor is a woman who, as a child, survived Auschwitz. Aged 10, she and her twin sister Miriam were imprisoned at Auschwitz where Dr Josef

Mengele used them for medical experiments. They both survived, liberated on 27 January 1945, but Miriam died in 1993 as a consequence of the experiments done to her as a child. No one else from Eva's family survived the war.

Over time, Eva was able to contact other twin survivors and exchange memories – something she found very healing. Later still she found the courage and strength to forgive the Nazis and, specifically, to forgive Dr Mengele. In doing so she says 'I felt the burden of pain was lifted from me. I was no longer in the grip of hate; I was finally free.' 'I had the power now…the power to forgive. It was my right to use it. No one could take it away from me.' (Cantacuzino, 2015)

The day Eva forgave the Nazis, she also, privately, forgave her parents whom she had hated for not saving her from Auschwitz. She had expected her parents to protect her but now realised that they could not have done so. Then she forgave herself for having hated her parents. Eva has gone on to write and speak publicly about her own experiences of forgiveness.

Desmond Tutu is the South African born cleric who played a major public role in opposing apartheid. South Africa was a country of 'internalised racism, inequality and oppression.' (Tutu, 2014) There were protests; there was violence; atrocities were committed. In 1993 apartheid finally came to an end, and in 1994, South Africans democratically elected Nelson Mandela as their first black president.

It was widely feared that the transition to democracy would become a bloodbath of retaliation. But, people chose to seek forgiveness rather than revenge. President Mandela appointed Desmond Tutu to head a Truth and

Reconciliation Commission, a commission focused on restorative justice, tasked with investigating and reporting on the atrocities committed by both sides in the struggle over apartheid. The victims of human rights violations were invited to give statements about their experiences, and some were selected for public hearings. Perpetrators of violence could also give testimony and request amnesty from both civil and criminal prosecution.

In 2003, a journalist, Marina Cantacuzino, in response to the imminent invasion of Iraq, collected stories from ordinary people who had lived through violence, injustice or tragedy and had sought forgiveness rather than revenge. In 2004 she founded The Forgiveness Project a 'charitable organisation that uses personal narratives to explore how ideas around forgiveness, reconciliation and conflict resolution can be used to impact positively on people's lives'. (Cantacuzino, 2015)

American born Megan Feldman Bettencourt is a journalist and author who, in 2015 wrote *The Triumph of the Heart: Forgiveness in an Unforgiving World*. Being a self-admitted holder of grudges, her interest in forgiveness was triggered by her introduction to Azim, a man whose only son had been shot and killed during a robbery. He had forgiven the man who had killed his son, and seemed to be at peace. Intrigued by Azim's attitude that 'there were victims at both ends of that gun', Megan began a quest to understand the complex concept of forgiveness, drawing on the latest scientific research and humanitarian perspectives.

What forgiveness is and what it is not

Based on our right as human beings to live in the present without the pain of the past, Eva Kor describes forgiveness as a deliberate act of self-liberation; an active decision to voluntarily let go of what was done. As Nelson Mandela said on his release after 27 years of imprisonment, 'As I walked out of the door toward the gate that would lead to my freedom, I knew if I didn't leave my bitterness behind, I'd still be in prison.' (Feldman Bettencourt, 2015)

In agreement with Eva Kor, Desmond Tutu describes the process of forgiveness, at an individual level, as being driven by the desire to no longer be defined by what was done to us or by what we did, facing the stark truth of what happened and moving towards acceptance of what was done. At a broader, humanitarian level, he describes forgiveness as being 'the way we return what has been taken from us and restore the love and kindness and trust that had been lost – bringing peace to ourselves and to the world'. (Tutu, 2014) Marina Cantacuzino adds that forgiveness is not about excusing others' or our own behaviour, but instead 'embracing human frailty and fallibility and taking responsibility for a society we have helped to create'. (Cantacuzino, 2015)

People who forgive can often be viewed by others as either saintly or spineless, the first being humanly unattainable and the latter definitely undesirable. Until more recent experience taught her otherwise, Megan Feldman Bettencourt used to view forgiveness with disdain seeing those who forgave as feeble and almost pitiable. But, the reality of forgiveness is far from this. Forgiveness is neither an attitude of the weak nor is it the privilege only of the divine; it is a skill that we all possess that requires incredible determination and strength.

Forgiveness involves neither forgetting nor condoning what was done, but centres instead on having the courage to face and accept the truth of what happened. In many cases, forgiveness is neither quick nor easy to achieve; sincere unconditional forgiveness requires consistent hard work and commitment.

When first introduced to the concept of forgiveness, Mia saw it as a religious obligation, something she felt she ought to be able to do because she felt it was the morally right thing. However, after much research and reflection, she began to see the sense of power over her own life that forgiving might provide.

Duncan, on the other hand, saw forgiveness as a sign of weakness, a sign of 'letting them win'. He really struggled with the thought of letting his resentment go and was a little afraid of who he might become without his anger – it was such a motivational force for him. He understood the massive challenge that forgiving would be for him, but again, having read around the subject and thinking about the consequences of not forgiving, he came to the decision that he would benefit by forgiving people from his past who had harmed him.

Having read the above, what does 'forgiveness' mean to you?

In relation to how experienced you currently are at forgiving, what past things have you forgiven?

What past things have you been forgiven for?

What past things have you forgiven yourself for?

We each have the individual right not to forgive; it's a very personal decision. But, should you choose not to forgive, there are, of course, consequences – consequences that affect not only you, but others too.

Consequence One: The likelihood of remaining defined by what was done, living in the past, unable to live fully in the present. If you have been harmed, you can get stuck in victimhood and inaction, unable to reclaim your story and re-cast yourself as the champion of your future. If you have harmed, you can get stuck in guilt, self-blame, shame and inaction.

Consequence Two: The emotional consequences of harming others or of being harmed are strong. Emotions such as rage, hate, terror, desire for revenge, blame, guilt and shame are but a few. These strong emotions trigger the body's stress response system, releasing chemicals such as adrenalin and cortisol through the body. If experienced for a prolonged period of time, this can have a damaging effect on the smooth running of the physical body, hindering our health and our immune system.

Megan Feldman Bettencourt discusses the 'science of forgiveness' citing research projects undertaken by Dr Frederic Luskin and Dr Robert Enright on the physical effects of forgiveness on medical patients. Quoting Dr Frederic Luskin, co-founder of the Stanford Forgiveness Project 'When you don't forgive you release all the chemicals of the stress response. Each time you react (to the memory of the offence), adrenaline, cortisol and norepinephrine enter the body. When it's a chronic grudge, you could think about it twenty times a day, and those chemicals limit creativity, they limit problem solving... (they) cause your brain to enter... the 'no-thinking zone', and over time, they lead you to feel helpless like a victim.' Luskin also found a significant link between patients who chose not to forgive and depression, anxiety and hostility.

Dr Robert Enright, a developmental psychologist who participated in the Campaign for Forgiveness Research demonstrated that cardiac patients with coronary heart disease who underwent forgiveness therapy were at less risk of pain and sudden death than those who received only standard medical treatment. (Feldman Bettencourt, 2015)

Consequence Three: Every individual has value; each one of us is an important human being. Yet it is our interconnectedness with others that gives our lives true meaning. (We are part of a family unit, a broader family, a social network, a community, a region, a nation, a continent, the world. We are human beings collectively.) What one person does can affect everybody. If rage and revenge are our chief motivators, it detrimentally affects not only us but all of those around us too.

Mia wanted to forgive. There were many people in Mia's life who had harmed her, but she wanted to begin by forgiving her father. She wanted a better, more fulfilling relationship with him. She yearned to move beyond that sense of powerlessness that she felt, and create a new life for herself, a life that she was in control of. She believed that forgiving her father was the best place to start this process.

As we know, Duncan was reluctant to forgive at first. He felt that, if he forgave, he'd be meekly giving in to what was. He wasn't sure that the people who'd harmed him deserved his forgiveness; he was so angry at the injustice of others' actions. However, he too came to the decision that he no longer wanted to be defined by his past experiences. Focusing on the sense of isolation from others that he felt, he wanted to start by considering the possibility of forgiving his birth mother whom he believed had abandoned him.

Do you feel that you might want to forgive or be forgiven? If so, why?

Who might you want to forgive or seek forgiveness from, and for what?

How do you anticipate your life will be once you have forgiven or been forgiven?

If you choose not to forgive or seek forgiveness, how might this decision impact your current and future life?

How will your relationships with others be affected by your decision to forgive or not forgive?

What constitutes 'a harm'?

We don't always get things right. Some of our interactions will go wrong and we will be hurt or we will hurt. But, what constitutes a wrong? We typically know the laws of the land in which we live. Our laws define specific wrongs – the law is pretty black and white. Plus, within each culture, each society, there are commonly accepted norms surrounding rights and wrongs: it's wrong to lie, to cheat on your partner, to bad-mouth a friend behind their back.

And then, things get a little less clear cut. As we grow and experience life, the things that happen teach us our own personal 'rules' concerning appropriate codes of conduct/rights and wrongs. We accept these rules as facts and expect others to follow them as we follow them. However, others have different life experiences and form their own codes of conduct that inevitably differ from ours. So, what one person considers is a serious transgression may be of little consequence to another.

What could prevent forgiveness?

1. The desire for revenge

For every state law broken, there is a punishment meted out to the perpetrator by the state. Our legal system, as it stands, underlines the concept of punishment as both a deterrent and as a means of retribution for a crime committed. This influences our understanding of what justice is; crime and punishment are associated. So, at an individual level, when someone harms us, the tendency is to seek revenge, to make the offender pay. An eye for an eye. Justice.

Thoughts of revenge (wanting to hurt the offender back) can act as a motivator, an energy that makes living after the offence worthwhile. Duncan was one of these people. But, in seeking revenge, we tend to hold the original offence in the forefront of our minds, causing us fresh pain, hatred and suffering every time we remember it. And, remember the physical damage hatred does to our bodies (the anxiety, the nausea, the exhaustion).

What was done to us was unfair, unjust and we have every right to be outraged, but hurting back rarely satisfies. At best, retaliation will give us only momentary respite from our pain and is likely to result in other uncomfortable emotions such as guilt and shame – in enacting revenge we place ourselves at the same level as the offender. Given that we are all capable of causing harm to others, this eye for an eye approach, as Mahatma Gandhi so clearly stated, will 'leave us all blind'. Think back to South Africa, just after the ending of apartheid, would the quest for revenge have benefitted the South African nation?

2. **Guilt**

We may feel that the offence we have committed is so heinous that we do not deserve forgiveness. To have transgressed our own codes of conduct and caused harm to another is a difficult fact to face – we often expect so much more of ourselves than we do of others. Guilt holds us in that time and space in which the offence was committed and can lead to isolation, self-destructive behaviours, and feelings of depression and anxiety.

When we've hurt someone else, there is a tendency to believe that we've done something bad therefore we are bad. The way forward is to begin to understand that we are all imperfect people who deliberately or inadvertently hurt others. It's about separating our behaviour from who we are as a person, understanding what we did and acknowledging the pain and suffering we caused to the other. We can choose to learn from this experience to make sure we don't repeat the same mistake and then, ideally, seek forgiveness from the hurt party. Even if forgiveness isn't granted to us, we can work towards accepting what we did, putting the lessons we learned in place and allowing ourselves to move forward and develop as a human being by forgiving ourselves.

Desmond Tutu believes 'there is nothing that cannot be forgiven, and there is no one undeserving of forgiveness.' (2014)

3. The desire for recognition and repentance from the offender
We might feel more inclined to forgive on a conditional basis, that is, if the offender recognises the pain they've caused, repents and apologises. But, such a requirement hands power back to the offender. Unconditional forgiveness is forgiveness with no strings attached. It removes any authority the offender might still have over us because, for us to move on, we need nothing more from the offender.

4. Secondary gains
We might be unwilling to forgive because we're unwilling to release the attention that being a victim affords us, or unwilling to release the 'weapon' that the harm has become against the perpetrator. Perhaps we believe, at some level, that the anger we feel after the offence is protecting us from worse emotions such as pain. Maybe we are loath to seek forgiveness because we feel our guilt is justifiable punishment.

What might stop you from forgiving or seeking to be forgiven?

How do we forgive?
Based on the approach adopted by the Truth and Reconciliation Commission, whether the offence committed

was of monumental significance or was more moderate in nature, I take my clients through a five-stage process of forgiveness. I now invite you to consider it.

Stage one: Detailing the facts of the offence – telling your side of the story

If we want real forgiveness, real healing, we first face the stark reality of the real injury. This initial stage requires the strength, willingness and ability to face the facts of what happened. It involves the detailing of the specifics of the harm that was caused because, when you understand the clear, hard facts and hold them to the light for further investigation, you can begin to make some sense of what happened.

(It's important to take a moment here, to note that every person's understanding of reality is different, and that re-telling the hurt will not necessarily represent the absolute truth of what was. Memory is not a faithful record of a moment in life, instead, memories are reconstructions of events, and are coloured by other memories and events. Memory is fallible; this is a fact. But, the way in which we have experienced and stored events is what's impacting our current life, therefore, our perception of the harm is what's important at this stage.)

Where her father was concerned, Mia felt that he'd failed in his duty as a parent to protect her from harm. In her eyes, not only had he left her, he had also sided with an adversary, his new wife, and, in so doing, had neglected to prioritise his daughter's needs. She blamed him for retaining the family home and for 'forcing' her, her siblings and her mother into inhospitable accommodation. She also held him responsible for her inability to know what to do in the face of conflict. Mia felt that her father had let her down.

Duncan felt a deep-rooted sense of abandonment by his birth mother. He knew none of the details of the adoption that took place; there was a dark void where the specifics were concerned. His imagination filled in the gaps. He believed that he had been an unwanted, ugly baby, a terrible mistake, and so was rejected soon after birth.

If you have been involved in 'an offence', what are the specifics of the harm? Write down all the facts about the transgression as you remember experiencing them.

Stage two: Examining the emotions caused by the offence

This stage is about detailing how the offence affected us, identifying the emotions it generated and giving those emotions names – rage, grief, pain, anxiety, fear, guilt, shame and so on.

Mia felt such anger towards her father for not managing to work through the relationship difficulties with her mother, and rage at being forced by her father to leave the family house and live in a place that bore no resemblance to home. Mia also felt a degree of shame where her parents' divorce was concerned – embarrassed by others knowing about the family breakdown. Having developed a high degree of empathy, she felt guilty that she might have somehow caused the divorce: 'if only I had been a better daughter'. She was afraid of her stepmother and worried about what Marlene might do next. She felt powerless and began to see life happening around her and to her. She came to understand that life was unstable, uncertain and a frightening place to be in. However, as she grew, this realisation helped her to recognise that, if she wanted her needs to be met, she'd have to meet them herself; her sense of self-reliance began to emerge and she became driven and ambitious to succeed (although her fear of conflict and desire to avoid it remained).

Where his birth mother was concerned, Duncan felt a deep-seated sense of loss and rejection. He was outraged at the injustice of his mother's abandonment of him, and felt such shame at being born unwanted – it was his fault that he was born unlovable. Duncan learned that he didn't quite belong and experienced a sense of isolation from the rest of humanity.

What emotions did the offence generate within you? Consider what the weight of these emotions is, and how you, your life, your world-view has changed as a result of what happened.

Stage three: Seeing the other side of the story

There are four aims to this phase of the forgiveness process:

- To put the offence into context.
- To begin to see things from the other's perspective, separating the person from what they did.
- To learn from the offence.
- To acknowledge what needs to be done to make amends.

What was it that led you or the other person to offend? What is your and their background story?

What part did each of you play in the offence?

If you are the harmed party, how would you have behaved had you been in the offender's shoes?

With the benefit of hindsight, what could have been done differently? What other options were open at the time?

Are there other ways to explain/alternative interpretations of the offence that was committed?

If you are the hurt party, separating the person from the harm they inflicted, how do you feel toward the person who harmed you? Is it possible for you to separate them from their actions?

Through this process we can begin to accept what happened and so begin to open our minds to what we learned from the experience. When we learn, we reduce the risk of repeating the same mistakes.

What did you learn from this offence?

It's often easier to forgive or be forgiven if the offender seeks to atone for the harm they caused.

What is it you require or what is required of you, to make amends for what was done?

Stage four: To forgive or not to forgive, that is the question

As I said at the beginning of this chapter, forgiveness is a choice, not a requirement. Having considered all the above, spend a moment or two just reflecting on how you feel about the possibility of now letting this harm go.

There's no need to make a decision yet, instead, leave your mind ajar to the possibility and wait to see how you feel whilst being guided through Audio 7a – Exploring the possibility of forgiveness.

N.B. If we choose to forgive, how will we know we truly mean it? This will be different for everyone who forgives or is forgiven. Some clients have described feeling as though a massive burden had been lifted, others as though they suddenly felt clean, no longer sullied. Many have described forgiveness as a sense of peace, a grace, an awareness of calm within themselves generated by letting something very cumbersome go. Others have experienced a feeling of acceptance of what happened and a readiness to move forward in their lives.

If there is someone you might want to forgive, or someone you might want forgiveness from, cue Chair Therapy Audio 7a – Exploring the possibility of forgiveness.

Mia's story: Rather than exploring the possibility of forgiving her father through Chair Therapy, Mia decided to meet with him face-to-face. She asked her father out for dinner. When he remonstrated that he 'couldn't come out without Marlene', Mia explained to him the importance of her request, and, with reservations, he agreed to meet. It took a while for Mia's father to take on board what she was saying and, at first, he denied her version of events. However, Mia calmly stuck to her message and one by one, her father's self-protective barriers came down. He was able to listen to her words and understand what they meant to her. His regret was palpable; he was able to acknowledge her pain and apologise for his 'failings' as a father.

After he had listened to her, Mia was able to give her father the chance to explain his actions. She learned that he had experienced a difficult childhood, being one of five children. His own father had been a man of his time and was absent from family life for much of the time. His own paternal role model had been a poor one, and he had very little understanding of what a father was other than providing for the family financially. Mia's father was regularly smacked for misbehaving and, where conflict was concerned, had learned to keep his head down. When Mia was five, her father took on board a very demanding job and was fatigued and irritable at the end of each day. When the divorce happened and it was decided that the father remain in the family home, Mia discovered that it had been her mother's decision to leave – her mother had insisted that she no longer wanted to remain in a place in which she had felt such misery. Once Mia's father had re-married, he had so wanted this new relationship to work that he buried his head in the sand and became blind to what was actually happening. He regretted all these things.

On hearing her father's explanations of why he had behaved in the ways that he had, Mia's understanding of this flawed individual grew and she felt empathy toward him. The knowledge of how things had been for him allowed her to walk a while in his shoes, and she realised that, given who he was, her father had probably done the best he could with the skills and abilities that he had at the time.

To begin to make amends, Mia wanted her father to acknowledge the mistakes that he had made and to apologise for them. She also wanted reassurance from him that, in relation to their present and future relationship, he would no longer prioritise Marlene's well-being over hers.

Although neither forgetting what her father had done, nor condoning his behaviour, she was able to whole-heartedly forgive him. She described this act as 'cleansing her inside and out'.

Duncan's story: Duncan did not know who his birth mother was and had decided not to make enquiries to seek her out; a face-to-face meeting was not possible to arrange. So, we devoted an entire session to Chair Therapy in which he imagined a one-to-one conversation with his mother:

Duncan was able to imagine his birth mother and what she might say that could explain her decision to give him up. He pictured a woman in her late fifties with a deep sadness in her eyes. He gave his imagination free rein, unhindered by the logic of the conscious mind. His birth mother, as he saw her, was dressed demurely, with a string of pearls around her neck, her hair mid-length and somewhat unkempt. Duncan imagined that the pearls had been inherited on the death of his mother's mother, the only thing that she had been bequeathed. The lady who sat before him had disgraced her family; she had become pregnant aged fifteen having been swept off her feet by a local married man. The shame that this brought to the family was intolerable and she was forced to leave the area for the duration of the pregnancy to stay with distant relatives. It was decided on her behalf that the baby be given away and that the incident never be spoken of again. The young mother never recovered from her loss and remembered her long-lost child every day of her life.

Duncan simply needed to give voice to his grievances and expose his pain to the daylight and for those grievances and pain to be heard. After he had said all he wanted to say to her, he invited his mother to acknowledge and apologise for the pain her actions had caused. He was able to imagine her doing this and, as a result, he felt like a terrible weight was lifted from him. His imagination had allowed Duncan to picture his mother's desire to keep him and enabled him, for the first time, to feel a sense of self-worth. Imagining this scenario engendered such a feeling of empathy toward his birth mother that Duncan was able to instantly forgive her. He described the feeling as 'utterly liberating'.

Now that you have listened to the Chair Therapy Audio 7a, Exploring the possibility of forgiveness, write down all that transpired. Have you forgiven or been forgiven? What are the likely consequences of this for you and for others in your life?

If you have decided to forgive or have been forgiven

Forgiveness represents the end of something old and the beginning of something new. During my years as a therapist

I've come to understand that the marking of such events can be incredibly beneficial and can represent a symbolic 'moving on'. It is for each individual to identify the most appropriate way in which to do this but, for example, the simple opening of a window can symbolise the exchange of old air for the new, or, the deliberate shutting of a door can represent closure, the opening of the door representing a beginning. Some of my clients have chosen to light a candle or plant a beautiful flowering plant in a meaningful spot of their garden to then nurture on a regular basis, whilst others have written the name and description of the offence on a piece of paper and then burned it.

Mia chose to mark her joy at having forgiven her father by throwing caution to the wind and spending money on herself, getting her hair re-styled, while Duncan sat quietly in his bedroom at his adoptive parents' house, looking at the adverts of properties to rent; he was ready to begin to take charge of his life.

If you have chosen not to forgive or not to be forgiven: understand why you have made this choice and what the likely consequences will be, and accept your right to have decided thus.

Is there anything you would like to do that could symbolise you having forgiven, having been forgiven or deciding not to forgive?

Stage five: Renewing or releasing the relationship
If you decided the relationship is worth renewing, it's important to understand that this does not mean going back to how things were prior to the transgression. The fact is that what happened changed things. It's now about

making a new relationship with that person, a relationship that acknowledges and accommodates the harm that was caused.

If you decide to release the relationship, it is understood within that decision that you wish the other no harm, but choose no longer to have them in your life (or they choose no longer to have you in their life). Such a choice is a valid one.

Mia chose to renew her relationship with her father. She saw this as a work in progress and took small steps where he was concerned, accepting his phone calls, and meeting up for family meals every now and then, hugging him hello and goodbye. Her father suggested a big family holiday, but Mia felt that this was too soon, and thanked him for his suggestion but said she wasn't ready for that yet. He accepted her decision.

Duncan had already decided not to try to find his birth mother. This is the decision that he stuck to.

Is your relationship to be renewed or to be released? What are the likely consequences of this decision?

Forgiveness of self

We are all regularly called upon to forgive each other – it's the nature of being in relationships. But, it's often harder to forgive ourselves; we have broken our own codes of conduct and this can really sting.

Forgiveness of self is every bit as valuable as forgiving others and being forgiven by others. Megan says: ' While blaming others is linked to anger and hostility, chronic self-blame is correlated with high anxiety, depression and negative self-esteem' (2015). She explains that those who showed self-compassion by forgiving themselves were able to better cope with stress over time.

Irrespective of whether you have been forgiven by the person you harmed or not, the process of self-forgiveness follows a similar path to the one described above:

- Acknowledge the truth of what you did.
- Identify the emotions caused by what you did.
- Put the offence into context.
- Accept responsibility but understand why you did it.
- Allow yourself to feel the regret and the remorse.
- Allow yourself to feel the desire to not repeat the same mistake.
- Acknowledge the lessons that you learned.
- Seek to make amends for the offence if it's possible.
- If you are ready to do so, and if it feels right to do so, choose to move forward by forgiving yourself.

Is there anything you want to forgive yourself for?

If so, cue Chair Therapy Audio 7b – Exploring the possibility of forgiving myself.

To re-cap: Forgiveness is a choice. It neither condones what was done, nor excuses the harm caused. What forgiveness offers is the opportunity of freedom from the pain of the past – physical and psychological liberation. As Desmond Tutu encourages: 'Forgive others, not because they deserve forgiveness, but because *you* deserve peace.'

Progress report:

My expectations: You have made your choice where forgiveness is concerned and accept the consequences of this decision.

What you've learned:

How this knowledge affects your perception of that old discomfort and dissatisfaction:

Chapter 10

How well do you really know yourself?

Who the bally-hoo-heck am I? It's an age-old philosophical question that has stimulated thousands of years of debate, disagreement and discussion.

Inscribed on the entrance to ye olde Oracle of Delphi in Greece are the words 'KNOW THYSELF', yet we often avoid the self-reflection that acquisition of self-knowledge requires, deriding it as navel-gazing, and so end up knowing other people better than we know ourselves. Our culture plays a role in this attitude; when I was growing up in 1960s Britain, to indulge in self-focus was deemed self-indulgent, almost immoral. But, we have come a long way since those days, and my work has taught me that accurate knowledge and acceptance of ourselves as unique individuals is fundamentally important to a healthy, happy and fulfilling life. It positively influences our self-respect, self-belief and self-confidence. Plus, when we feel good about ourselves, like those ripples on the pond, people around us also benefit.

Our identity, who we are, is an on-going process of development; we are permanently learning and adapting ourselves. Being aware of who I was and considering who

I might become are as important as knowing who I now am. I am a very different person now to the shy, woe-is-me teenager who left secondary school (thank goodness), and I'm sure, in 10 years' time, I'll be a different person to the woman I am today. Yet knowing myself as I am now enables me to choose a future for myself that is most likely to provide me with the greatest satisfaction. With greater self-knowledge comes the opportunity for wiser decision-making.

Influenced by the culture and period of history into which we're born, our experiences, memories, values, personalities, beliefs, thoughts and feelings are crucial aspects of how our identities develop. Beneficially or otherwise, they influence the many choices we make in life including our careers, friendships and relationships, voting patterns, whether we have children or not, where we live and so on.

The questions posed in previous chapters will have helped you reflect on who you once were and how you came to be that person. The following questions serve to help you identify the nitty-gritty of who you are *now*, not who you were a few weeks ago; *when you're addressing each question, let go of those old self-definitions.* Again, I advise you to *take your time* and tackle only a few questions per day; the more time you invest in this part of the process, the more you are likely to gain from it.

N.B. It's great to learn about ourselves, but this knowledge has little value if we neglect to use it. When you have a greater understanding of who you are, reflect on how you can use this information to improve your life and your sense of wellbeing. For example, I know that I thrive on contact with those near and dear to me. So, despite my busy schedule, I make sure to take time to be with my loved ones.

From a current perspective, take your time to really consider each category below and rate your typical, day-to-day levels of being:

	Not at all				Very much
Relaxed	1	2	3	4	5
Curious	1	2	3	4	5
Sociable	1	2	3	4	5
Ambitious	1	2	3	4	5
Sensual	1	2	3	4	5
Complicated	1	2	3	4	5
Old	1	2	3	4	5
Creative	1	2	3	4	5
Quiet	1	2	3	4	5
Secure	1	2	3	4	5
Optimistic	1	2	3	4	5
Irritable	1	2	3	4	5
Anxious	1	2	3	4	5
Suspicious	1	2	3	4	5
Conventional	1	2	3	4	5
Self-reliant	1	2	3	4	5
Trusting	1	2	3	4	5
Angry	1	2	3	4	5
Analytical	1	2	3	4	5
Weak	1	2	3	4	5
Imaginative	1	2	3	4	5
Punctual	1	2	3	4	5
Judgemental	1	2	3	4	5

	Not at all				Very much
Respected	1	2	3	4	5
Attractive	1	2	3	4	5
Fraudulent	1	2	3	4	5
Playful	1	2	3	4	5
Aloof	1	2	3	4	5
Disciplined	1	2	3	4	5
Shy	1	2	3	4	5
Reflective	1	2	3	4	5
Tolerating	1	2	3	4	5
Intelligent	1	2	3	4	5
Loved	1	2	3	4	5
Critical	1	2	3	4	5
Co-operative	1	2	3	4	5
Healthy	1	2	3	4	5
Contented	1	2	3	4	5
Unforgiving	1	2	3	4	5
Affectionate	1	2	3	4	5
Focused	1	2	3	4	5
Extrovert	1	2	3	4	5
Helpful	1	2	3	4	5
Risk taker	1	2	3	4	5
Loud	1	2	3	4	5
Innovative	1	2	3	4	5
Religious	1	2	3	4	5
Political	1	2	3	4	5
Feminine	1	2	3	4	5
Afraid	1	2	3	4	5

How well do you really know yourself?

	Not at all				Very much
Principled	1	2	3	4	5
Rational	1	2	3	4	5
Manipulative	1	2	3	4	5
Lazy	1	2	3	4	5
Excited	1	2	3	4	5
Sad	1	2	3	4	5
Jealous	1	2	3	4	5
Kind	1	2	3	4	5
Satisfied	1	2	3	4	5
Self-deprecating	1	2	3	4	5
Practical	1	2	3	4	5
Adult	1	2	3	4	5
Appreciative	1	2	3	4	5
Fun-loving	1	2	3	4	5
Stressed	1	2	3	4	5
Reliable	1	2	3	4	5
Domestic	1	2	3	4	5
Committed	1	2	3	4	5
Aimless	1	2	3	4	5
Physically fit	1	2	3	4	5
Adaptable	1	2	3	4	5
Addicted	1	2	3	4	5
Concerned	1	2	3	4	5
Negative	1	2	3	4	5
Grateful	1	2	3	4	5
Interesting	1	2	3	4	5
Competitive	1	2	3	4	5

	Not at all				Very much
Hold grudges	1	2	3	4	5
Sexual	1	2	3	4	5
Assertive	1	2	3	4	5
Procrastinating	1	2	3	4	5
Needy	1	2	3	4	5
Self-critical	1	2	3	4	5
Fulfilled	1	2	3	4	5
Decisive	1	2	3	4	5
In the moment	1	2	3	4	5
Happy	1	2	3	4	5
Deferential	1	2	3	4	5
Demanding	1	2	3	4	5
Distracted	1	2	3	4	5
Masculine	1	2	3	4	5
Short-term	1	2	3	4	5
Hard working	1	2	3	4	5
Controlling	1	2	3	4	5
Empathetic	1	2	3	4	5
Aggressive	1	2	3	4	5
Valued	1	2	3	4	5
Depressed	1	2	3	4	5
Blaming	1	2	3	4	5
Obsessive	1	2	3	4	5
Balanced	1	2	3	4	5
Inadequate	1	2	3	4	5
Confident	1	2	3	4	5
Supportive	1	2	3	4	5

How well do you really know yourself?

	Not at all				Very much
Greedy	1	2	3	4	5
Motivated	1	2	3	4	5
Emotional	1	2	3	4	5
Easily bored	1	2	3	4	5
Perfectionist	1	2	3	4	5
Selfish	1	2	3	4	5
A push-over	1	2	3	4	5
Prejudiced	1	2	3	4	5
Clumsy	1	2	3	4	5
Satisfied	1	2	3	4	5
Irrational	1	2	3	4	5
Positive	1	2	3	4	5
Forgiving	1	2	3	4	5
Regretful	1	2	3	4	5
Interested	1	2	3	4	5
Truthful	1	2	3	4	5
Catastrophising	1	2	3	4	5
Goal-driven	1	2	3	4	5
Communicative	1	2	3	4	5
Determined	1	2	3	4	5
Black and white	1	2	3	4	5
Green/ecological	1	2	3	4	5
Good in a crisis	1	2	3	4	5
Strategic	1	2	3	4	5

With reference to the above, describe your personality.

Thinking about who you are in relation to the world around you and with reference to such things as your sex, gender identification, age, ability/disability, social status, class, educational background, geographical location, political and religious persuasion and so on, further describe who you are.

Detail the main events/people that have had an influence on who you have become.

List your top 10 qualities/strengths. Now choose someone who knows you well and ask them to also make a list of your top 10 strengths. Compare the two lists. Having compared the two lists, what, if anything, do you now know about yourself that you didn't know before?

List your weaknesses. What impact do these weaknesses have on your current life?

Thinking about who you are in relation to other people around you, what roles do you play in life? For example: Father/mother, husband/wife/partner, sister/brother, carer, manager, friend, provider, volunteer and so on.

How important/valued/respected do you feel in each of these roles? What are the implications of this?

With the roles you play in life in mind, list your 'needs'. For example: As a wife/husband/partner, you may need to feel respected and loved; to be treated as an equal; to be encouraged and stimulated; to be satisfied sexually; to have fun, and so on.

Are these needs being met and what are the implications of this?

List and explain your values/moral/ethical principles.

Over time, we all develop personal 'rules/codes of behaviour' that we try to live our own lives by; we often expect others to live by them too, as though they were common law. List your own, personal top 10 'commandments'.

List the interests/activities you enjoy doing and describe why you enjoy doing them.

Describe your appearance and your comfort/discomfort with how you look.

What are your achievements to date?

What, if anything, have you achieved/overcome that you didn't think you could?

What makes you feel happy? What makes you laugh?

What makes you feel sad? What makes you cry?

If any, what are your current problems?

Complete the following sentence 'I feel most alive when...'.

For example: 'I feel most alive when I'm dancing (free style).' But, let's be more specific: First, what does it mean to feel alive? From my perspective, being totally present, completely in the moment, enables me to know and feel I'm alive. Second, what is it about dancing that helps me feel so alive? It's a lack of concern about others' judgement; a sense of connection, connecting to something bigger and more powerful than myself; a feeling of sensuality and movement; excitement; the joy of there being no rules to obey – the freedom of letting go.

Having identified the details of what helps you feel alive, how can you bring more of these elements into your everyday life?

When you reflect on your life in the present, what do you feel content with?

When you reflect on your life in the present, what do you feel discontent with?

When you reflect on your life to date, what do you feel grateful for?

To summarise:

Complete the following statement: I am ...

What do you like and value about yourself?

How far do you accept yourself for who you are?

What, if anything, are you willing to change?

What are the likely benefits of making these changes?

What resources do you have and/or help will you need to make these changes?

To re-cap: As individuals we are learning and adapting ourselves all the time. But, by knowing who we currently are, we are giving ourselves the best opportunity to make choices that will benefit our lives in the present and in the future.

Progress report:

My expectations: You now have a much clearer understanding of who you are, and will apply this knowledge to benefit your daily life.

What you've learned:

How this knowledge affects your perception of the discomfort and dissatisfaction you used to feel:

Chapter 11

Summarising progress to date

I extend my hearty congratulations to you for getting to this part of the change process. No doubt you will have gone through some ups and downs, but I hope you now feel better off for all your hard work.

What I expect you to have gained from this book so far is:

- An appreciation of how the mind generates our behaviour and the understanding that the vast majority of what we do is automatically driven by the unconscious mind.
- An understanding of what hypnotherapy is and how clinical hypnotherapists use hypnosis (the trance state) to generate change.
- A recognition that people can and do change; that you can change; that you *have* changed.
- That you are now 'at cause' in your life.
- That change is an opportunity to rise to and that you have the resources to handle it.
- That change can be challenging to those around us (who may try to sabotage our efforts).

- That making mistakes is part of the learning process; mistakes help us develop.
- That pretty much every long-term problem carries with it secondary gains.
- That knowing how change fits into the bigger picture of your life aids commitment.
- How to set viable goals.
- How to deal with internal conflict through parts therapy.
- How to control your physical and emotional response to a given situation through the 5/7 breathing and through your anchor.
- An understanding of the value of healing past unresolved issues through regression.
- A recognition of the significance of beneficial core beliefs.
- An appreciation of the value of forgiveness and the process by which you can forgive.
- A much clearer understanding of who you are and how you can use this knowledge to enhance your life.
- An acceptance that you are now starting to live your life the way you want it to be.

To be learned:

- The value of self-reliance through self-hypnosis.

To summarise and cement all that you've learned so far, just lie back, relax and listen to Audio 8: Bridging the past and the future – enjoy!

Write down all that you can remember about what came to mind whilst listening to the recording.

On a scale of 1-10 with 1 being hardly at all and 10 being very, how uncomfortable and dissatisfied do you now feel?

Progress report:

My expectations: If you feel that your level of discomfort has reduced markedly to around the 0-2 range, marvellous! If, however, your level of discomfort scores a 3 or more, just spend a little time reflecting on what it is that's still causing the discomfort, and use self-hypnosis (Chapter 12) to continue to work at it.

Where you are:

Chapter 12

My gift to you – self-hypnosis

Self-hypnosis, the act of hypnotising oneself, is the final step in the process of change that I teach to all my clients. It is a multi-purpose technique that can be used every day of our lives, tailoring the experience to meet our exact requirements. Amongst other things, it enables each person I work with to see that they are not dependent on me or anyone else to guide them through further problem-solving issues. *Self-hypnosis promotes self-reliance.*

There are many similarities between meditation and self-hypnosis, the main difference between the two being that self-hypnosis tends to have a goal in mind, something specific to achieve – problem solving, choosing between options, overcoming a habit, de-stressing, re-framing a situation. Meditation, on the other hand, is typically, although of course not exclusively, orientated toward emptying the mind, freeing the mind of thoughts.

There are multiple ways in which self-hypnosis can be applied. It enables us to gain direct access to our own unconscious mind and gives our imagination free rein. For example, at a physical level, it allows us to rest, repair and strengthen the body, boost the immune system, speed up the healing process, re-balance the mind and body. At a psychological level, self-hypnosis can be used to re-programme the mind to overcome detrimental habits and behavioural responses, to tune into our wisdom to find solutions to specific issues, to use our creativity to think through options, and our observational skills to see things in their true perspective. Basically, its applications end where our imagination stops.

Many, many people have done and do use self-hypnosis on a regular basis. Not surprisingly, I am a big fan. To ready myself to be the very best that I can be, I use self-hypnosis to focus my mind before each client arrives for their session. I also regularly indulge in self-hypnosis to counteract the rationalising and analysing that I do, giving my mind much needed time-out to waft about in the ether. My haven is a place I visit often – it's inspirational. And, I'm in good company; Albert Einstein, the world-renowned German-born theoretical physicist, was known to perform self-hypnosis every afternoon, allowing his imagination to flow freely. Reportedly he came up with his theory of relativity during one of these sessions. It has also been widely noted that Winston Churchill used self-hypnosis, his goal being to manage the sleep deprivation that he experienced during the peak of World War II.

The process of self-hypnosis is not complicated. All hypnosis is, in effect, self-hypnosis, in that you *allow* yourself to enter the trance state; you are already well versed, therefore, in taking yourself into trance. You can do it.

There are 10 simple steps:

1. Find a quiet, warm, safe place in which to relax, where you won't be disturbed.

2. Decide how much time you have available. (Initially, perhaps set an alarm clock in an adjacent room to build confidence in your ability to bring yourself out of hypnosis at the desired/required time.)

3. Tell your mind what it is you want to achieve – perhaps a specific problem to solve, or boosting your understanding of your own natural abilities and confidence; perhaps simply a desire to benefit from deep relaxation.

4. Close your eyes and take a few deep breaths – the 5/7 breathing. Give yourself permission to relax, trusting in your own mind to achieve what you set out to achieve.

5. Imagine yourself at the top of your flight of steps and immerse all your senses in what emerges (details will vary from time to time). Understand that your haven rests at the bottom of the tenth step.

6. Count yourself slowly down each of the steps. With each step down, feel your body relaxing, releasing more and more, your mind calming, entering that blissful state of hypnosis.

7. At the bottom of the tenth step your haven emerges, that place of safety and beauty where peace, comfort, creativity and wisdom reside. Again, immerse yourself

in all the details of your haven (aspects will probably vary from one session to another).

8. Become aware of the comfortable chair within your haven and slowly drift over to it. Recline in its softness. Feel the safety, the security as you lie there. Pull the warm blanket of relaxation over your body and allow the conscious mind to drift to wherever it chooses to drift, understanding that the unconscious mind can then attend to the task in hand.

9. Emerging: When you feel that the time is right (something you will become adept at with practice), pull the warm blanket of relaxation away from your body, slowly get up from the chair and walk towards the staircase.

10. Remind yourself that, with each step up, you will become more and more alert, until at the top of step one, your eyes will open, you'll be fully aware and refreshed, but still calm and relaxed.

🎧 Cue Audio 9 – Learning the art of self-hypnosis

Progress report:

My expectations: You are more comfortable with yourself and with your life, and have the skills and abilities to self-direct problem solving from now on.

Where you are:

For future regular use: Audio 10 – Self-hypnosis (simply music).

The next stage

Informed by Audio 8, Bridging the past and the future, and by visualisations you can carry out while in self-hypnosis:

If any, what new opportunities are open to you now, opportunities that you might not have seen before?

What are your current goals?

Putting your life in the context of future possibilities, and with your goals in mind, where do you see yourself in 12 months' time?

In conclusion

After completion of their change processes, both Mia and Duncan remained in sporadic contact, wanting to share with me their latest achievements. Mia went back to college and is now a part-time teaching assistant. Her relationship with Geoff and her two daughters has its ups and downs but, on the whole, is far more satisfying than it was. Mia and her father are closer than they've been for a long time. She now chooses when to drink wine, no longer feeling the compulsion to do so. But, most empowering of all is the belief she now has in herself; trusting her own judgement, she now makes decisions and is willing to take responsibility for the outcome of those choices. She is comfortable. She accepts herself, flaws and all.

Duncan was able to move out of his parents' home and into accommodation that he shares with two others. His social life has expanded and he's in a satisfying intimate relationship with a person he met whilst at a friend's house for dinner. He left his place of work and is now employed in a far more satisfying job. He's thinking about finding his birth mother. He now feels at ease in his own skin, connected to others and free to enjoy life. He likes who he is becoming.

Mia and Duncan are works in progress, as are we all.

I'd like to thank you for reading this book. I hope you have found it both interesting and useful, and that you feel able to re-visit any aspect of the development process should the need arise. I trust that your experiences of following this book have enabled you to gain more of an an understanding of how you came to be the person you were, and to feel a greater sense of comfort with who you are now and who you might become in the future.

I wish you well in all that you do from this point on. Become who you choose to be.

References

Beck, J. S. and Beck, A.T., *Cognitive Behaviour Therapy: Basics and Beyond* (Guilford Press, 2011)

Bernard, M.E., *Rationality and the Pursuit of Happiness: The Legacy of Albert Ellis* (Wiley-Blackwell, 2010)

Cantacuzino, M., *The Forgiveness Project: Stories for a Vengeful Age* (Jessica Kingsley Publishers, 2015)

Eagleman, D., *The Brain: The Story of You* (Canongate Books, 2015)

Dryden, W., *Overcoming Anxiety* (Sheldon Press, 2000)

Fallon, J., *The Psychopath Inside: A Neuroscientist's Personal Journey into the Dark Side of the Brain* (Penguin, 2014)

Feldman Bettencourt, M., *Triumph of the Heart: Forgiveness in an Unforgiving World* (Hudson Street Press, 2015)

Goldberg, S., *Texts in Developmental Psychology: Attachment and Development* (Arnold, 2000)

173

James, O., *Not in Your Genes* (Penguin, 2016)

Tutu, D. and M., *The Book of Forgiving* (Collins, 2015)

Wiesel, T.N. and Hubel, D.H., 'Single-cell responses in striate cortex of kittens deprived of vision in one eye', Journal of Neurophysiology, June 26, 1963

Wolinsky, S., *Trances People Live: Healing Approaches in Quantum Psychology* (Bramble Books, 2007)

Script sources:
Allen, R.P., *Scripts and Strategies in Hypnotherapy: The Complete Works* (Crown House Publishing Ltd, 2004)

Hammond, D.C., *Handbook of Hypnotic Suggestions and Metaphors* (The American Society of Clinical Hypnosis, 1990)

Havens, R.A., Walters, C ., *Hypnotherapy Scripts: A Neo-Ericksonian Approach to Persuasive Healing* (Brunner-Routledge, 2002)

Hudson, L., *More Scripts and Strategies in Hypnotherapy* (Crown House Publishing Ltd, 2010)

Jaye, B., *The Wall*

Martin, N., Institute of Clinical Hypnosis

Audio music:
 'Silk Blanket' composed by Charles Vald